D0231418

The Dictionary of Tourism
First Edition

Edited by Charles J. Metelka

Merton House Publishing Company, Wheaton, Illinois

First Edition 1981

ISBN: 0-916032-10-8
Library of Congress Catalog Number: 80-83526

Merton House Publishing Company
937 West Liberty Drive
Wheaton, Illinois 60187

Manufactured in the United States of America

Introduction

Tourism has emerged as a distinct and impressive discipline. Practitioners have entered the field from a variety of backgrounds, each using a professional vocabulary that applies, in part, to the phenomenon variously known as tourism, hotel administration, restaurant management, hospitality, and the travel industry.

The boundaries of contemporary tourism are far from being identified, and even farther from being agreed upon. While it is understandable that each practitioner has an individual viewpoint on tourism, this parochialism has limited the development of a tourism vocabulary to a number of glossaries. Increased recognition of tourism as a world-wide phenomenon makes it important that persons wishing information on the terms used in the discipline have access to a reference work that is not so limited.

To be sure, a number of disciplines and professions have been popularly defined as tourism; even the casual observer tends to equate it with airlines, hotels, and travel agencies. In a larger sense, however, tourism is first and foremost a human activity that has some categories of business associated with it. Hotels are not tourism even if some percentage of their occupancy is derived from tourists. Airlines are not tourism; they are merely a contemporary facilitator, as were once the railroad and steamship. Tourists do not need travel agencies *per se*; they need information. Nevertheless, because this dictionary is a reflection of the tourism industry as it exists today, the user will find that transportation and travel agency terms predominate. One must not confuse the businesses associated with tourism with tourism itself, for the businesses only provide contemporary service to a phenomenon that transcends any one form.

Tourism is a human activity that, by its nature, draws from many established disciplines but transcends any one of them. The study of tourism must begin with the issues, problems and potentials of tourism itself rather than with efforts to extend the limits of the traditional disciplines. While tourism is not geography, history, architecture, law, economics, transportation, or sociology, the knowledge of these and other disciplines contributes to what we already know as well as to what we seek to discover.

A varied and increasing number of professionals recognize tourism as part of their domain. Hoteliers, travel agents, restaurateurs, city planners, insurance actuaries, environmentalists, and marketing experts among others, owe some or part of their livelihood to tourism. Those who choose the career of tourism professional must in turn be familiar with a myriad of existing disciplines, at least to the extent that they know enough to know that they don't know. The tourism professional may be thought of as a coordinator, sensitive to the many specialties needed for success and able to communicate effectively with each specialist. Recognition of this need to communicate in many ways is perhaps most apparent when one reads the front pages of many tourism destination area newspapers. Tourism is at once a commercial, economic, social, and cultural dynamic force; it may be thought of as an impressive example of human cooperation.

The task of compiling a dictionary of tourism terms was at once frustrating and satisfying. Frustration took many forms; words are patently inaccurate and limiting when used to describe a human activity as old as humanity itself, global in variety, and interplanetary in aspiration. Every effort has been made to provide definitions that transcend the editor's own preferences and biases.

Entries were selected from among words and terms that 1. are in contemporary use by more than once part of the tourism industry; 2. are frequently used and considered important by at least one part of the tourism industry; 3. are specific to tourism; 4. are used in the academic study of the theory of tourism.

While comprehensive, the dictionary is inevitably far from complete. Trade associations were entered only if they were national in scope for the United States and multinational outside the United States. Cities and established destination areas and attractions were not included. Federal government agencies somehow involved in tourism are at best sampled, as this list alone would be unending. Similarly, only a sampling of activity options have been provided for this too would constitute an infinite list. One final category of content omissions should be noted: while it is evident that numerous geographic locations conjure up strong tourist images, it was not thought necessary to duplicate existing tourism geography texts.

The Dictionary of Tourism was developed in the hope that its entries, definitions, and even its omissions will serve to advance the study and practice of tourism by disseminating and encouraging discussion and creative disagreement. The author and the publisher will welcome additions and corrections for inclusion in later editions.

This dictionary exists only because of the encouragement, patience and assistance of many people too numerous to enter here. However, recognition must be given to Jafar Jafari, who has been a strong supporter of the project since its inception and to Leland Nicholls, who reviewed the initial entries. Special appreciation is reserved for my wife, Kathleen, and for the publisher, Laurence Stevens, whose ability to motivate by use of both the carrot and the stick approximates an artform.

Charles J. Metelka
University of Wisconsin-Stout

A

AAA *See* American Automobile Association.

AAR *See* Association of American Railroads.

ABA *See* American Bus Association.

aboard On a ship, aircraft, train, or other mode of transportation.

abroad In or traveling to a foreign country.

absorption Practice in which a transportation or accommodation supplier accepts the lesser of two rates when a difference between the regular rate and a lesser rate exists due to published special requirements. For example, an airline will accept or in effect absorb the difference between a regular fare and a lesser fare caused by computing a joint fare.

access roads *See* feeder roads.

accommodation capacity *See* hotel capacity.

accommodation industry General term encompassing the many forms of commercial accommodations.

accommodations Lodgings of any sort for the traveler. *Commercial* lodgings are paid for—in effect rented—from someone who provides this service for a fee. *Noncommercial* accommodations include vacation or second homes, user-provided tents or campers, or staying with friends or relatives.

acculturation Merging of two or more cultures as a result of contact and interaction. Not always equal—one culture may be modified or submerged to conform to the culture of the dominant society.

accuracy in menu Consumer and industry movement to increase the precision of all descriptions of food items on a restaurant menu with regard to origin, extent of prepreparation and the like. The industry prefers the term "accuracy in menu" over "truth in menu" as the latter carries connotations of untruth. *See* truth-in-advertising legislation.

acid rain Precipitation in the form of rain or snow containing a higher than normal level of acidity. The condition is caused by urban industrial pollution reacting with water molecules in the clouds. Acid rain is a tourism concern because it tends to raise the acidity level of lakes and streams, thereby killing fish and adversely affecting the ecology. The major tourism recreational areas of the north central and north eastern United States are particularly sensitive to this problem.

acquisition Purchase, in entirety or controlling interest, of one company by another.

activities host/hostess Employee of a hotel, resort, or cruise ship, responsible for arranging, overseeing, and sometimes encouraging the guest or passenger to take part in the activities offered as entertainment options. On a ship, called *cruise director.*

ACTOA *See* Air Charter Tour Operators of America.

actual flying time Total amount of time one is actually in the air, computed from take-off to landing, for one flight or as a total of a number of intermediate flights from one point to another.

adjoining rooms Adjacent rooms but with no connecting door between them. *See also* connecting rooms.

advertised tour Preplanned itinerary or travel program described in a brochure. An Inclusive Tour (IT) number is assigned to a tour that includes air transport and that meets specified airline requirements. *See also* IT number.

aeronautics Science and art of flight.

affinity group Membership organization, formed for some purpose other than travel, which may decide to sponsor group travel programs. Schools, businesses, trade associations, religious groups, clubs, and numerous other organized membership entities are defined by the CAB as affinity groups.

agency Office or other location of a retail travel agency.

agency representative Salesperson representing an airline, tour operator, hotel, and so forth, calling on travel agents.

agency tour *See* familiarization trip/tour.

agent In general, a person authorized to act for, or sell the products or services of, a supplier. A *retail travel agent* is an employee of a retail travel agency authorized to sell accommodations, transportation, and other tourism-related services to individuals and groups. A *ticket agent* is an employee of a carrier who solicits, obtains, or arranges for air transportation for individuals or groups; also known as a *counter salesperson* or *ticket salesperson.*

agricultural tourism Arrangement to give the client an experience of farm or ranch life and environment.

AGTE *See* Association of Group Travel Executives.

AH&MA *See* American Hotel & Motel Association.

AIEST *See* International Association of Scientific Experts in Tourism.

Air Charter Tour Operators of America (ACTOA) Association of charter tour operators.

aircraft Any contrivance used or designated for navigation or flight in the air. A *fixed-wing* aircraft may be propelled by either piston engines or gas turbine (jet engines); a helicopter derives its lift from revolving blades (rotor) on a vertical axis and can hover and land and take off vertically; a *vertical takeoff and landing* (VTOL) aircraft can take off and land vertically or in a short distance; a *supersonic transport* (SST) is capable of a normal cruising speed greater than the speed of sound (741 mph at sea level). Within each aircraft category, or series, there may be other designations. For example, a propeller-driven aircraft may be powered by either a piston (internal combustion) engine or a gas turbine (jet) engine; the latter are called *prop jets* or *turboprops.* A *stretch jet* is an aircraft where the manufacturer has left the original design relatively intact but designed a longer fuselage so the aircraft might carry a larger payload. A *wide-body* aircraft is the generic term applied to the new generation of aircraft designed to carry large numbers of passengers.

aircraft, civil Any aircraft other than a public aircraft and other than those owned by the United States Government.

aircraft, convertible Aircraft that may be converted from passenger cabin configuration to cargo cabin configuration by removing the seats. *See also* configuration.

aircraft grounding Voluntary or required order to refrain from flying an aircraft. Reasons for grounding range from actual malfunction to poor weather conditions. In cases of actual or suspected serious malfunction, the Federal Aviation Administration may order the grounding of one aircraft, or some or all of a particular type of aircraft.

aircraft piracy Seizing or taking control of an aircraft by actual or threatened force or violence. Also called *hijacking*.

airline codes *See* codes.

Airline Deregulation Act of 1978 Law amending the Federal Aviation Act of 1958; it provides for a phased end to the CAB's regulating authority over domestic airlines by 1985.

Air Line Pilots Association (ALPA) Trade union representing airline pilots.

airline representative Salesperson or account executive representing an airline and calling on travel agencies, commercial accounts, or other organization that have the ability to produce substantial business for the airline.

Air Line Stewards and Stewardesses Association (ALSSA) Trade union of airline flight attendants.

air mile International air mile, a measure of distance equaling approximately 6,076 feet. *See also* nautical mile; statute mile.

airport Area used for takeoff, landing, storage, and maintenance of aircraft. The term *airfield* is used interchangeably, but usually denotes a smaller-sized facility; *jetport* usually means an airport with long runways for use by jet aircraft.

airport art Handicrafts made exclusively for sale to tourists, generally mass-produced and having little value beyond that of souvenirs. Also called *junk art*.

airport code Three-letter code identifying airports nationally and world wide. Examples: ORD = O'Hare International (Chicago); LAX = Los Angeles International.

Airport Operators Council International, Inc. (AOCI) Worldwide trade association of governmental bodies that operate airports.

airport transfer Service sometimes offered by hotels free for guests, providing transportation to and/or from the area's airport either on demand or according to frequent schedule.

air-sea   Travel programs or itineraries using some combination of both air and sea transportation.

air taxi   Aircraft carrying up to 19 passengers. *See also* air taxi operator.

air taxi operator   Company operating aircraft within 250 miles of its home base using aircraft carrying up to 19 passengers.

air terminal   Structure on the grounds of an airport where departing and incoming passengers are processed.

Air Traffic Conference (ATC)   Division of the Air Transport Association responsible for setting standards and establishing agreements that regulate the activity of domestic airlines, among themselves, with international carriers and with the travel industry in general.

air traffic hub   Cities and standard metropolitan statistical areas requiring aviation service. An air traffic hub can be small, medium, or large, determined by the community's percentage of total enplaned passengers in scheduled and nonscheduled service.

Air Transport Association (ATA)   Trade association formed in 1936 to promote business by serving as an information center for industry planning. Represents virtually all scheduled airlines in the United States.

á la carte   Each food item on the menu is ordered, prepared, and priced separately.

alcove   Small space set off from some larger area or room, usually used for sleeping.

all-expense tour   Tour offering all or most services for an inclusive price. Terms and conditions of the tour contract must specify all the tour arrangements and services paid for and included as prepaid.

all-in   British term for all-inclusive tour arrangements.

ALPA   *See* Air Line Pilots Association.

ALSSA   *See* Air Line Stewards and Stewardesses Association.

ALTA   *See* Association of Local Transport Airlines.

altiport   Field or area suitable for landing aircraft in a mountainous region.

ambient resource   One or more qualities of a destination area that make it attractive for tourism, including climate, scenery, interesting culture, or other features.

amenities   Services offered by a hotel, restaurant, or other tourism business or resort area or other tourism entity; the basic amenities for an airline: modern aircraft, efficient staff, and so forth are assumed to be present and are not mentioned. Subtle amenities tend to be noted in advertising as a reflection of the quality of the company, again for an airline, hot towels, flowers for each lady, and so forth.

American Automobile Association (AAA)   Membership association offering insurance programs, emergency road service, and trip planning.

American Bus Association (ABA)   Trade association.

American Hotel & Motel Association (AH&MA) Lodging industry trade association.

American Motor Hotel Association (AMHA)   Trade association.

American plan (AP)   Hotel accommodations with three meals daily included in the price of the room. In Europe, called *full pension. Modified American plan* (also called *half pension)* is a rate that includes a room, breakfast, and either lunch or dinner.

American Sightseeing International   International trade association of local tour operators.

American Society of Travel Agents (ASTA)   Trade association of United States travel agents and tour operators. International and allied memberships for trade-associated industries are also offered.

AMHA   *See* American Motor Hotel Association.

Amtrak   Name used by the National Railroad Passenger Corporation, a semipublic corporation formed in 1971 and charged with managing and rejuvenating United States intercity passenger railroad service.

amusement park   *See* theme park.

antipodean day   Day gained by crossing the 180th meridian when traveling eastward; also called meridian day. *See also* international date line.

AOCI   *See* Airport Operators Council International, Inc.

AP   *See* American plan.

aparthotel   *See* hotel garni.

appointment, agency   Process whereby travel agencies are approved by conferences to represent a group of carriers, or by a company, hotel, or other supplier to represent and sell its services.

architectural preservation   Process of identifying, saving, and restoring old buildings and structures of historic, cultural, or nostalgic value.

ARTA   *See* Association of Retail Travel Agents.

artifact   Manmade object valued as representing the culture of the craftsperson.

Association of American Railroads (AAR)   Trade association.

Association of Group Travel Executives (AGTE)   Trade association of group travel operators and promoters.

Association of Local Transport Airlines (ALTA)   Trade association of local service airlines in the United States.

Association of Retail Travel Agents (ARTA)   Trade association of travel agents in the United States.

ASTA   *See* American Society of Travel Agents.

astronomical day   24 hours of solar time measured from noon to noon.

ATA   *See* Air Transport Association.

ATC tour order   Standard form covering only the sale of advertised air tours that have been authorized by the Air Traffic Conference.

atmosphere   Pervading emotional quality of a place or a group of people.

attitude   Tendency to behave in an expected way; cluster of assumptions that cause people to draw conclusions or make up their minds.

attraction   1. *Man-made* attractions are physical structures (Statue of Liberty, Empire State Building) or events (Olympic Games); 2. *Natural* attractions are physical phenomena deemed unusual and/or beautiful (Grand Canyon, Alps); 3. *Secondary* attractions have tourist appeal, but are not the primary reason for visiting a location.

attractive nuisance doctrine   Legal doctrine that when an object or item (for example, a swimming pool) is dangerous and of a nature which might attract children, it is the obligation of the business to anticipate that children will be attracted to the danger.

automated reservation system   Computerized system offering a travel agent or large commercial account direct access through an in-office terminal to airline, hotel, or tour computers. Each system varies slightly from the other, but all include a keyboard to gain access to the computer and to make reservations, a cathode ray tube (CRT) for visual display of flight availability and other necessary data, and a printer to print tickets and itineraries. Complete business systems (including accounting) are available with some systems.

Automated reservation systems include APOLLO (United Airlines); MARSPLUS (ITT Electronic Travel Services); PARS (Trans World Airlines); SABRE (American Airlines); SYSTEMAC (Air Canada).

automatic guide   Prerecorded tape and battery-operated tape-player to be used as an information source. Printed books and maps may supplement the machine. The tape is linked with the area to be visited on foot or by automobile, with a specific starting point and instructions on when to stop the tape, where to look, and when to go on. May also be used in stationary installations in parks and museums, offering accurate explanations of exhibits and displays.

automobile club   Association that offers its members numerous travel-related services and benefits, including world-wide trip planning, insurance, emergency road service, and so forth. The American Automobile Association (AAA) is an independent association; some major oil companies also provide these services.

automobile rental   *See* self drive.

available seat mile   One aircraft seat available for sale, whether occupied or not, transported one mile. The statistic is obtained by multiplying the number of available for-sale seats on a given aircraft by the number of miles flown by that aircraft.

average room rate   Charges for each available room in a property, during a season, or at a destination, added together and divided by the total number of rooms.

B

B&B   *See* bed and breakfast.

back bar   Supply and storage cabinets and countertop located behind the bartender in a bar service operation.

back of the house   Those portions of a hotel, motel, restaurant, or other facility that are not in direct contact with the guest/customer under normal conditions. For example, the payroll department and food preparation areas.

back-to-back   Method of operating tours or flights on a consistently continuing basis. For example, a flight arriving with passengers would immediately board another group of passengers, either for a return trip or for a continuing flight. Also, the hectic situation in which customers are departing at the same time as others arrive.

baggage   Traveling bags and personal possessions of a traveler. In travel terms, *accompanied baggage* is that carried in the same vehicle as the passenger; *unaccompanied baggage* is carried separately. *Checked baggage* is handed over by the passenger, to be claimed at the destination; *unchecked* (or *carry-on*) *baggage* stays in the passenger's possession.

baggage allowance   Per-person amount of baggage by total weight, number of pieces, or volume that will be transported without additional charge.

baggage check   Receipt or claim ticket for accompanied baggage, issued by a carrier.

baggage claim area   That part of a transportation terminal where passengers may claim baggage checked in at departure rather than carried on as accompanied baggage. *See also* carousel.

baggage, excess   Passenger's luggage that exceeds stated limitations in weight or size, and requires payment of a separate fee for carriage.

baggage insurance   Usually, optional supplementary insurance against baggage loss or damage, requested and purchased by the traveler.

balance of payments   Statement of international monetary transactions; the amount of money leaving a country for goods and services, as opposed to that coming in. Historically, tourism contributed to a deficit in the balance of payments in that United States citizens spent more money abroad than foreigners spent in the United States. More recently, decline in the value of the dollar has led to more foreign travel spending in the United States.

banquet room   Often part of a hotel, providing a paying group with a private area, the necessary service personnel and prearranged amounts and varieties of food and beverage service.

bar   Place of business that sells liquor by the drink to customers, many or all of whom sit on stools or stand next to the counter (or bar) upon which the drinks are made and placed.

bareboat charter   Boat, yacht, or other vessel rented without supplies or crew. *See also* provisioned charter.

bargaining   Process of negotiating the price of a product or service between the seller and a would-be buyer.

barrier-free   Designation for a building, service, or area designed to permit use by the physically handicapped.

barriers   Factors that hamper or prevent a person from traveling. Such barriers include lack of sufficient funds, lack of sufficient time, physical handicaps, fear, language differences, family stage, and lack of interest or knowledge.

barter   Exchange of goods or services not involving exchange of money.

basing point   Geographical location or point to and from which fares are established, and used in calculating fares to and between other points.

beach operator   Sea, ocean, or lakeside business—either independent or a service of a hotel or resort. Umbrella, cabana, or surfboard rentals, or instruction in various crafts or activities, may be offered by beach operators.

bed and breakfast (B&B)   Room rate that includes either English or Continental breakfast; used primarily in the United Kingdom and Europe, but also in some parts of the United States.

bed-night   Statistic based on one person spending one night in a hotel or motel.

bedroom   Room for sleeping, especially when part of a suite; on railroads, a compartment for two persons with separate toilet and washing facilities.

bedroom suite   1. In a hotel, accommodations that include a separate sitting area or room in addition to a bed; 2. On railroads, two adjoining bedrooms with the common or separating wall removed, which sleeps four, also called a *double bedroom.*

bell captain   Hotel employee who schedules and supervises bellhops.

bellhop   Employee of a hotel who carries a guest's luggage to the assigned room after a guest has checked in, and who often explains the features of the room.

Bermuda plan (BP)   Hotel accommodations with a full, American-style breakfast included in the price of the room.

berth   1. Sleeping and sitting bed arrangement on a ship or train where upper and lower beds (berths) are attached to a wall. They may fold when not in use. *See also* railroad classes of service (U.S.A. and Canada); 2. Space where a ship may dock.

best available Supplier's promise to provide the best possible accommodations for a client. When part of a request for a reservation, it means that the client desires and will pay for the best accommodations available in the property.

bilateral agreement Written treaty between two nations agreeing to reciprocal air services in accordance with details of equipment, scheduling, taxation, safety standards, and other factors as specified by both countries.

bill of fare List of the foods served in a restaurant; also called a menu.

bistro Business establishment offering live locally-known entertainment, a dimly lit romantic atmosphere, liquor service, and sometimes light meals. A night club.

black market Business transactions that violate the law. May involve currency exchanges.

block booking *See* blocking.

blocking Practice of wholesalers to reserve a number of rooms or transportation seating far in advance, with the intention of selling the rooms or seats as part of tour packages.

blue peter Letter "P" flag of international code. It gets its name from the color—blue with a white square center. Flown by a vessel expected to sail within 24 hours.

board To go on board a ship, aircraft, or other transportation vehicle.

boarding house Small units for rental on a weekly, monthly, or seasonal basis, which are usually part of a larger, older home that has been partially opened to paying nonfamily members. The fee usually includes all meals. Also known as a *guest house* or *pension. See also* tourist home.

boarding pass Card given to a passenger just before boarding an airplane or other carrier. It indicates that the passenger has completed all check-in procedures, and also designates the seat and section to be occupied. On ships, an *embarkation card.*

boat Small open craft propelled by oars, sail, or engine. *See also* ship; dinghy; yacht.

boatel Commercial accommodations similar to a motel in services, but designed for customers traveling by private boat.

boat landing Public, private, or commercial ramp arrangement permitting the launching and removal of watercraft, especially watercraft towed by automobile.

bond Guarantee of financial protection for suppliers and clients, purchased by a premium paid by an agent or operator to a bonding or insurance company.

bon voyage French term of farewell. *Bon voyage parties* are usually major celebrations held before departure when traveling a significant distance.

booking *See* reservation.

booking form Document completed by the purchaser of a tour that provides the tour operator with needed information about the purchaser. It also contains a legal statement of what specifically is being purchased.

BP *See* Bermuda plan.

break-even analysis Statistical tool used in decision-making, whereby fixed and variable costs, sales projections, and pricing alternatives are systematically varied to identify the best combinations.

break-even point Important analytical tool for any business. The point at which revenues equal fixed and variable costs. Below the break-even point losses are incurred; above it, profits are made.

briefing tour Hotel or visitor's bureau promotion. Usually sells the destination to the travel trade at the trade's location, as opposed to selling it at the destination.

brochure General term for printed promotional literature offered by tourism businesses.

brown bagging Practice of customers bringing their own liquor into an establishment not licensed to sell liquor. In most cases (restaurants) the action is legal as only sale is forbidden; in other cases the practice may be illegal but socially expected and acceptable (sports events).

BTD *See* business travel department.

bubble car *See* dome car.

budget hotel Commercial accommodation facility that stresses low rates, usually possible because only necessary rather than luxury services are provided.

buffet Style of food service. Also, the display table of the already prepared foods, to be selected as well as transported by the customer to the eating area. A common arrangement at large gatherings.

bum boat Small boat used to bring peddlers to a ship to sell merchandise and souvenirs to the passengers.

bump To remove or displace a passenger or guest in favor of someone who has a higher priority.

bumper sticker Message-carrying sign for attachment to the rear bumper of a car. A form of souvenir.

bungalow *See* individual housing.

bus 1. Large motor-driven vehicle in scheduled or chartered service. Often called a *motorcoach* when used for tours; 2. Act of clearing used restaurant tables and moving the dirty dishes to the washing area.

business travel Travel that is the result of one's occupation. In the case of conventions or where a side trip is added to what would otherwise be strictly business, pleasure may also be involved. Business travel involves a special market requiring some special services (typists, meeting rooms) and expectations that differ from those of the purely-for-pleasure tourist.

business travel department   Business firm's in-house travel agency.

buyer's market   Supply-demand condition where excess amount of product (airline seats, hotel rooms) puts the buyer in control. Often leads to lower prices, extra services, or wider selection. *See also* off season.

CAAA   *See* Commuter Airline Association of America.

CAB   *See* Civil Aeronautics Board.

cabana   Hotel room, with or without beds, usually set apart from the main building and situated in a pool or beach area. Also, a temporary structure used for the same purpose, or for a special event.

cabin   1. Sleeping room on a ship, usually less luxurious than a stateroom; an *outside cabin* has a porthole and is preferred over an *inside cabin,* which has no view; 2. Passenger compartment of an aircraft; 3. Separate structure in a rustic setting for rent by customers. *See also* stateroom.

cabin attendant   *See* flight attendant.

cabin lift   *See* teleferic.

cable transporters   A number of different types of people-moving machines for use at winter ski resorts. In each case a motorized cable, anchored at a base near the resort and at the top, where the downhill skiing begins, provides the means of transport. Types include rope tows, J-Bars, T-Bars, chairlifts, and cabin lifts.

cabotage fare   Special reduced fare, limited to citizens of a country traveling within the boundaries of that country.

café .Small restaurant; coffee shop.

camp counselor   Person employed to lead, direct, and instruct the users of a seasonal, recreational, or educational camping facility.

campground   *See* camping site.

camping site   Area for tent camping, motor home, or trailer use with sanitary services and in some cases, restaurants, vehicle service stations, and recreation facilities nearby. In Europe, called a caravan site.

cancellation fee   Amount to be paid by one who fails either to use reserved accommodations, or to cancel by some designated deadline.

capacity   Theoretical expectation that there is a physical limit to the amount of use or number of people a facility can service while maintaining the quality of the site and the experience.

captain 1. Person in complete charge of the operation of a ship or aircraft; 2. In a dining room, the waiter in charge of the other waiters; 3. In a hotel, the person in charge of some group of employees, as bellhops are responsible to a bell captain.

captain's table Dining room table hosted by the captain of a cruise or passenger ship. Other officers may also host tables.

caravan park European term for a campground or camping trailer facility. *See also* camping site.

car ferry *See* ferryboat.

cargo airline Air carrier authorized to provide scheduled freight services as well as nonscheduled operations that may include passenger operations.

cargoliner *See* freighter travel.

car hop Employee responsible for parking cars of arriving patrons and returning the car when the patron departs. Also, a style of waitress service in a drive-in restaurant.

carousel Mechanism that delivers checked baggage to the baggage claim area of an airport or railroad station.

car rental *See* self drive.

carriage Act of transporting passengers and cargo or freight, and the charge for such services.

carrier, designated air Airline of a nation that is specifically identified in a bilateral agreement to operate over a specific route between two nations.

carrying capacity 1. In transport, the passenger-moving potential of the vehicle; 2. In destination areas, the level of use that can be withstood before the quality of the experience deteriorates.

carry-on baggage *See* baggage.

cartography Map-making.

cash bar Private room liquor bar setup where the guests pay for their own drinks. Also known as a *no-host bar*.

casino Gambling establishment, usually part of a luxury resort complex.

catering Providing prepared food for the paying guest or customer. General term for any restaurant, buffet, or snack food operation. Also, a specific form of business/service where all necessary items including food, tables, chairs, utensils, and decorations are brought into a customer's home or provided at a facility for a group of people, invited by the customer, for a meal or party that is not open to the public.

ceiling 1. Theoretical maximum of a given statistical projection based on present trends and assumptions. The ceiling marks the point at which a forecast projection curve begins its descent; 2. Altitude at which the cloud cover begins.

Celsius Measure of temperature where the freezing point of water is 0° and boiling point is 100°. Formerly known as centigrade. *See also* Fahrenheit.

centigrade *See* Celsius.

Certificate of Public Convenience and Necessity Certificate issued by the Civil Aeronautics Board authorizing an air carrier to provide air transportation along specifically designated routes and in accordance with other specified restrictions.

certification *See* registration.

Certified Travel Counselor (CTC) Certificate of professional competence, attesting to a travel agent's successful completion of a study program developed and administered by the Institute of Certified Travel Agents.

chain Company that owns or has a financial interest in more than one unit/property. The underlying financial arrangement does not need to be advertised to the customers but in most cases the numerous units are promoted as such to stress availability and popularity.

chair lift Motorized moving cable with open chairs for one or more users, providing transport, designed for winter ski resort use but also functional in the summer for sightseeing. *See* cable transporters.

chalet *See* individual housing.

chamber of commerce Membership association of businesses in a local area that seeks to promote business to and within the area. The chamber of commerce acts as a clearing house of information for existing and prospective business people and area residents. Often serves as a tourism promotion bureau.

chart Sea or air map.

CHART *See* Council of Hotel and Restaurant Trainers.

charter To hire by contract the entire capacity or minimum number of seats of an aircraft, bus, ship, or train. There are many different types of charters. Examples include *pro rata charter* or *affinity charter,* for bona fide members of an organization not formed for the purpose of travel, the cost of which is divided equally among all participants; *single entity charter,* where the cost is borne by the charterer (person, company, or organization) and not by the individual passengers; *split charter,* in which the entire capacity of the aircraft is divided into groups (usually a minimum of 40) of seats among different charterers; *inclusive tour charter,* the hire of an aircraft, or block of seats, by a tour operator or travel agent for the carriage of persons traveling on inclusive tours that include hotel accommodations, sightseeing, meals, and other tour components. *See also* affinity group.

charter airline *See* supplemental airline.

charter boat Watercraft available for charter or hire by a person or group for any duration, and for a variety of purposes, including fishing and sightseeing.

charter flight   Scheduled or nonscheduled flight booked or contracted by one or more groups for their exclusive use, and meeting specified charter conditions. Such flights are usually less expensive than regularly scheduled flight services because charter conditions lead to a larger percentage of occupied seats. Also referred to as a *service charter*. *See also* charter.

chauffeur   Driver, often of a rented luxury automobile. Also, the act of transporting passengers short distances in a private vehicle for a fee.

check average   Statistic obtained by dividing the total amount of sales by the total number of customers during a specified time period.

check-in   Official registration and paperwork completed on arrival of a guest or passenger. This would include signing a register card at a lodging, or getting a boarding pass for some means of transport.

check-in time   Time at which a hotel or motel room is ready for occupancy. Also, the time at which a passenger should register arrival at a terminal prior to departure.

check-out time   Time by which a guest of a lodging is required to vacate accommodations to avoid additional charges.

chef   Head or main cook in a restaurant.

child   Variably defined in travel; the supplier sets the age limits for reduced fares and hotel rates. Child fares for air travel include anyone from 2 to 12 years of age. Some child rates, as in hotels and motels, are effective up to 14, 16, and even 18 years of age.

chit   Voucher for an amount owed for food, drinks, etc.

CHRIE   *See* Council on Hotel Restaurant and Institutional Education.

circadian rhythms   Physiological rhythms relating to the 24-hour cycle of the earth's rotation. The normal sleep, glandular, and metabolic rhythms of a person may still persist when traveling, resulting in the traveler being unable to quickly adjust to the new time zone. *See* jet lag

circle trip   Roundtrip journey whose outward and return routings are different.

city codes   *See* codes.

city lights   Tendency of rural youth to be attracted to the apparently superior way of life and excitement of an urban area.

city package   Package tour composed of transportation, accommodations, and sightseeing opportunities and any number of other tour elements, all in one particular city.

city pair   Terminal points of an air trip; the originating and destination cities.

cityscape   Total visual presence and impact of an urban area or destination area. Vantage points are often provided for visitors and residents so that they may experience the area on a grand scale and as an orientation for subsequent detailed use.

city terminal   Airline ticket office located elsewhere than at the airport, where passengers may check in, receive seat assignments, and get transportation to the airport.

city ticket office (CTO)   Sales office or counter of a carrier, located elsewhere than at the terminal.

city tour   Sightseeing package, usually including a motorcoach or other vehicle, and a guide. Important attractions and sights in and near the given city are included.

Civil Aeronautics Board (CAB)   The United States government regulatory body designated under the Federal Aviation Act to consider aviation matters affecting the public convenience and necessity, including supervision of routes, passenger and cargo fares, conditions of service, and schedules. Scheduled to be phased out January 1, 1985.

clearance   Permission to depart given by customs and health officials to ship or aircraft captains.

CLIA   *See* Cruise Lines International Association.

client   Customer of a business or travel agency.

climate   1. *Natural* climate is the weather conditions prevailing at a destination; 2. *Sociopsychological* climate is the attitudes and expectations of a certain group at a certain location—guests, employees or area residents.

closed dates   Time periods when everything available at a facility or service has been booked.

cluster development   Strategy of land use that locates a great variety of desirable services and activities in close proximity; not only more economical when land values are high but also exciting for the users.

CMTA   *See* Common Market Travel Association.

coach   In railroads, a car for ordinary daytime short-haul travel. In airplanes, the tourist class section. *See also* coach service, railroad classes of service (U.S.A. and Canada).

cocktail lounge   Facility that offers customers a place to have a drink in a relatively quiet, often dimly lit, atmosphere.

codes   Standardized abbreviations used by airlines, travel agents, hotels and others in the tourism industry to designate specific fares, types of service, cities, airports, etc. For example, LAX=Los Angeles; AP=American plan.

coffee shop   Commercial food facility designed to offer the customer a meal or a snack in an informal atmosphere without the service, variety, or cost associated with a restaurant, and at those times when a restaurant may not be open.

commercialization   Descriptive term indicating that virtually every activity, need, or desire of the visitor has been assigned a monetary value. Usually used in a negative context; everything from sun to smiles has been turned into a commodity for sale.

commercial rate   Special discounted rate offered by a hotel or other supplier to a company, individual, or other valued repeat customer.

commissary   Centralized kitchen capable of producing large quantities of food that is then delivered to and served at a number of locations.

commission   Amount of money determined by a percentage of the sale, paid by suppliers to travel agents for the sale of air transportation, hotel accommodation, tours, rental cars, and other products and services.

commission override   *See* override.

commoditization   *See* commercialization.

Common Market Travel Association (CMTA)   Association seeking to promote travel to and within the Common Market nations of Europe.

common rated   Situation where the fare from a specific point of origin is identical for two or more destinations because of the relative proximity of the destinations.

commuter airline   Air taxi operator that performs a minimum of five roundtrips per week between two or more points and publishes flight schedules of such services. *See also* air taxi operator.

Commuter Airline Association of America (CAAA)   Trade association of regional and intercity airlines.

compartment   Area on a ship, train, or airplane separated by walls of any type to create a private or distinct space. *See also* railroad classes of service (U.S.A. and Canada).

complimentary   Free; a product or service given without charge, often in recognition of repeated past patronage, a promise of future patronage, or to rectify some mistake. A night's lodging, a drink or a dinner may be complimentary. Often referred to as a "comp."

comprehensive development planning   Planning strategy for the continual readaptation and renewal of an area in recognition of present and future needs.

concentrated development strategy   Planned location of tourism facilities in limited areas, leaving larger areas relatively untouched.

concept facility   Lounge, hotel, amusement park, or some other building, room, or area designed to have a definite theme. Experiencing the total effect is a major reason for customer patronage. Often identifiable by its unusual name.

concession   Place of business on the grounds of an area that is not open to general business competition, as in the case of a state or national park. A concession is permitted as the result of successfully meeting certain stipulations, and perhaps successfully bidding for the privilege.

concierge   Employee in many major hotels, especially in Europe, in charge of guests' services such as baggage handling, dinner reservations, letter mailing, and other personalized services.

concourse Passageway for passengers and visitors in an airport leading to and from the terminal lobby and departure gates.

concrete jungle Derogatory term for an urban destination area appearing to be crowded, disorganized, and poorly managed.

conditional fare Airline tariff innovation aimed at reducing the loss of revenue caused by no-shows. The purchaser of a conditional ticket in essence buys a regular economy ticket, arrives at the airport, and gambles that the plane is full, in which case the fare is refunded and the person flies free on the next available flight. However, if there is room, the airline fills a no-show seat and the conditional fare purchaser pays for the trip.

conditions *See* terms and conditions.

condominium Once regarded simply as an apartment that a person owned rather than rented or as the building which housed such units. The term has expanded in meaning to include any multiple-ownership arrangement with or without buildings (ownership of trailer spaces and hookups, recreational facilities). *See* timesharing.

condominium hotel Hotel totally or partly comprised of individually owned condominium units. All or some of the owners have agreed to an arrangement that permits management to offer the units as hotel rooms at specified times of the year in return for a share of the revenue.

conducted tour *See* escorted tour.

Confederation of Latin-American Tourist Organizations (COTAL) Association of tourism promotional agencies of the Latin-American countries.

conference 1. Association of carriers formed to establish and administer rules to the benefit of its members. A conference may set fares and rates; allocate routes; establish and enforce rules, safety and ethical standards; regulate activities of travel agents and others who do business with member carriers; 2. Group meeting. *See* convention.

conference center Large facility designed to provide the space and services needed for groups holding meetings.

conference room Room of varying size rented out for group meetings.

confidential tariff *See* tariff, confidential.

configuration Arrangement of seats in a transport vehicle or aircraft cabin. The number and size of seats abreast in a row, and the seat pitch, are varied to provide different passenger densities for the classes of service available. *See also* seat pitch.

confirmation number Number provided over the telephone by the reservationist replacing or prefacing a mailed confirmation slip; also provided to confirm, in a case of erroneous billing, the approved cancellation of a reservation.

confirmation slip Printed document certifying that the holder does in fact have a confirmed reservation for a room, seat or some other reserved-space activity.

confirmed reservation Oral or written statement by a hotel, restaurant, airline, or other supplier that the request for a reservation has been received and will be honored. Reservations are confirmed within a context of binding limitations and obligations. For example, a hotel often requires that a guest arrive before 6:00 P.M. or chance the loss of the reservation.

congress *See* convention.

connecting flight A flight which requires the passenger to change aircraft as part of the itinerary.

connecting point Intermediate location in an itinerary where the passenger changes from one flight to another to continue the journey.

connecting rooms Two or more rooms with a private connecting door permitting access between the rooms without going into the corridor.

consignment Arrangement under which the seller retains title to merchandise until his agent sells it. Popular with craftspeople.

consolidator Person or company that negotiates travel plans for individuals or groups, for the purpose of creating charters.

consortium Group of persons or companies who pool their resources and money to invest in or purchase some entity that would be beyond the financial capabilities of any one of the group. Popular in the travel agency field for the purpose of earning override commissions and centralizing support services, such as accounting, advertising, and marketing functions.

Consumer Price Index Composite statistic developed and computed by the United States government that includes data on the price of travel. The travel price section of the index includes transportation, lodging, food, and entertainment away from home. Cost comparisons over time are possible by use of the index.

continental breakfast Light morning meal, usually consisting of a beverage and toast or rolls. *See also* English breakfast.

continental plan Hotel room rate that includes both the use of the room and a continental breakfast.

continuing space Parts of an itinerary still to be travelled. Also called *downline.*

contractor Person, firm, or corporation providing vehicles, guides, or local services to a tour operator or travel agent. Sometimes called *local operator, receiving agent, ground operator, reception agency, subcontractor,* or *land operator.*

convenience food Food that is partially or fully processed before its final preparation for consumption. Includes canned, frozen, and dried foods.

convention 1. Business or professional meeting, usually of large numbers of people. The term *congress* is a common term outside the United States; 2. An international agreement on a specific matter, especially the outcome of a meeting.

convention and visitors bureau Municipal or state organization responsible for promoting tourism to the area. Often funded by a combination of public and private money.

convention center Specialized facility designed to meet the needs of large groups of people with ample parking, large and small meeting rooms, banquet facilities, audio-visual equipment, etc. Often publicly funded for the purpose of stimulating the business of nearby hotels, motels, restaurants, and attractions, each of which could not afford to provide a facility of sufficient size.

conventioneer Person attending a convention.

conveyance Act or means of moving persons or goods from one location to another.

Cook, Thomas Born in England in 1808, Cook became the first known tour operator by arranging trips to temperance meetings in England.

co-op advertising Arrangement by which several sponsors combine to purchase advertising time or space, often with the benefit of greater impact and reduced cost.

core concept Design strategy for a hotel lobby, resort area, or so forth, which gives the user a central point of focus, attraction, or orientation. Also applied to the strategy of centrally locating kitchens, elevators, and so forth, to save construction expense.

cost-benefit analysis Multivariate statistical technique that identifies the probable outcomes of competing tourism investment strategies. Values must be placed upon the various costs and benefits that result from a given development strategy. Alternative outcomes can then be considered in light of the socioeconomic consequences each would have for the community or region.

COTAL *See* Confederation of Latin-American Tourist Organizations.

cottage industry Production of goods in the worker's home, a process usually requiring little capital investment or machinery.

couchette *See* railroad classes of service, (Europe).

Council of Hotel and Restaurant Trainers (CHART) Association of hospitality industry personnel directors.

Council on Hotel Restaurant and Institutional Education (CHRIE) Nonprofit professional association of schools, educators, industry professionals, students in the hospitality industry.

counter agent Ticket seller for a carrier.

coupon 1. Document issued by a tour operator or carrier in exchange for which travelers receive prepaid accommodations; also called exchange order or voucher; 2. Part of an airline or other ticket; the *flight coupon* is surrendered by the passenger at check-in; the *passenger coupon* contains the contract of carriage; the *agent's coupon* is retained by the travel agency; the *auditor's coupon* is submitted with the sales report. *See also* exchange order.

coupon payment "Open commissions" proposal whereby the amount paid to an agent by an airline for the sale of a ticket would be based on the fact of the sale rather than on the amount of the sale. Also called *flat rate coupon payment. See also* open pay.

courier *See* tour manager

cover Number of paying customers served food during one meal period.

cover charge Fixed fee for table service independent of the charge for the food. Usually imposed in night clubs or luxury restaurants offering entertainment.

credit card Method of consumer credit that initiates a transfer of funds from the person to the establishment which sold the goods or services to the person.

crossing the line Ceremony observed when a ship crosses the equator. Those who are crossing the equator for the first time are subjected to initiation ceremonies, "Father Neptune" comes aboard and holds court, interviewing the first-timers to see if they are worthy of being given a pass to cross the line. The passengers then go through the initiation ceremonies, which include ducking in the swimming pool and other lighthearted pranks. *See also* Neptune.

cruise Voyage for pleasure rather than for transport, usually departing from and returning to the same port.

Cruise Lines International Association (CLIA) Trade association of cruise lines seeking to promote cruises by offering education programs for travel agents.

CTC *See* Certified Travel Counselor.

CTO *See* city ticket office.

cuisine Style of cooking, either ethnic (as Spanish) or showing a particular approach (as *cuisine minceur*). From the French for kitchen, as in *chef de cuisine*.

cultural festival Celebration marking the importance of a historical date, character, or event.

culture Way of life of a society—customs, laws, mores, beliefs. *Culture conflict* results when members of several groups are in contact and competition. *Culture lag* results from uneven rates of change among parts of a culture. *Culture consciousness* describes the emphasis in a destination area on unique historical and cultural heritage, rather than on mass tourism features such as beaches or luxury hotels. *Culture shock* describes the disorientation experienced when a society experiences excessive change.

currency restrictions Limitations, procedural requirements, and other regulations established by a nation to foster or force a favorable balance of payments, by limiting the amount of funds residents can take out of the country, or by prohibiting the exchange of local currency for a departing visitor's home currency.

current demand Amount of sales or number of customers a business, activity, or attraction has at present. Current demand may also be determined for a specific type of customer or for a specific day, meal period, product or service.

customer-activated ticketing Proposed computerized funds transfer system whereby a customer would need only to insert a credit card and flight choice information in order to receive an airline ticket.

customer count   Number of revenue customers at a given function, event, or attraction during a specified period of time.

customer traffic   Number of separate sales transactions during a specific time period.

customs   1. Government required procedure whereby all persons entering the country must declare their possession of specific kinds or amounts of items. Persons returning after visiting foreign destinations are required to declare all foreign-purchased items. A tax or customs duty may have to be paid on some or all of the foreign-purchased items; 2. The usual way a group of people or a society behaves in a given situation. Differences in customs between tourists and residents may lead to unforeseen and unintended problems, as well as serve as a basis of attraction between the two groups, especially the tourist.

customs declaration   Official form and the process of specifying articles that have been purchased or otherwise obtained outside the United States of America and certifying that no prohibited items or substances are in one's possession. The United States Customs Service, a unit of the Department of the Treasury, administers the process to all persons—citizens and aliens—entering the United States.

customs duty   Tax on certain categories of goods imported into a country.

cut off date   Designated date by which additional specific action must be taken by a person who has reserved or blocked space in a facility, or face invalidation of the reservation. A tour operator may be required to submit the names of clients as well as full or partial deposit; individuals who have reserved a banquet room may be required to finalize their intentions by paying a nonreturnable deposit.

D

DATO   *See* Travel Industry Association of America.

Davy Jones' locker   Bottom of the sea.

day rate   Rate charged customers to utilize a hotel or motel room during the day only. Often a service of properties located near airports for use by passengers awaiting connecting flights. The day-rate guest must vacate the room in time for it to be resold at the regular rate.

day tripper   Person who tends to take one-day trips. Also, a person who takes one-day tours from one centrally located destination area, to avoid changing hotels.

deadhead   1. Aircraft or transportation vehicle operating without a payload of passengers or cargo; 2. Nonrevenue passenger, as in the case of an employee traveling on a pass.

dead reckoning Method of finding a ship's approximate position from the distance run and the course steered.

decor Components of a property that combine to create a socio-emotional feeling or atmosphere for the guest, tourist, or customer. Includes lighting, size, building materials, music, plantings, costumes, and so forth.

default Failure to perform the terms of a contract by a stipulated time.

deluxe Declared to be of the highest standard; when part of a hotel rating system, a property wherein all rooms have a private bath and a variety of services are available.

demand Quantity of tourism goods or services that buyers are ready to buy, at a specified price, in a given market at a given time.

demi-pension *See* half pension.

demography Statistical study of human populations with particular reference to birth and death rates, mobility patterns, age and sex composition, and other distributive factors.

demonstration effect Tendency for a more economically primitive culture to imitate the behavior patterns of a more complex culture. Also, the human tendency to learn from another person or group and to incorporate the learned behavior into one's own lifestyle.

denied boarding compensation Legally required penalty for not honoring a confirmed reservation, paid by an airline to a passenger.

departure tax *See* head tax.

deplane To leave an aircraft.

depletion Reduction in value of a once highly valued resource by overuse or improper care.

deposit receipt Written acknowledgement of initial payment received from a customer to reserve space for transportation, accommodations, or other services.

deposit reservation Hotel or motel reservation for which at least one night's payment has been received. The room must then be held for the first night, no matter how late the guest arrives. Also applies to any tourism business requiring or accepting advance payment to guarantee a space, room, seat, table, or whatever service is involved.

depot Terminal for commercial land transportation, as a bus depot, train depot. Also known as a *station*.

deregulation *See* Airline Deregulation Act of 1978.

destination Geographic location to which a person is traveling. The *final destination* is usually the farthest place away from the person's point of origin and/or the place where the person intends to spend the majority of time. An *intermediate* or *enroute destination* identifies a place where some shorter period of time is spent, be it for an overnight rest or to visit an attraction.

destination area development   Recognition of the interrelationship of social, economic, and physical aspects involved in developing a tourism destination.

DET   *See* domestic escorted tour.

deuce   Table for two people.

devaluation   Government decreed reduction of the number of foreign units of currency that can be obtained for one unit of the home (devalued) currency.

developing country   Also *underdeveloped* or *less developed* country. Refers not to cultural values but rather to economic or technological development. May also be used to refer to a country in the process of initiating a tourist industry.

de-velopment   Opposite of *development*. A community may opt to use a planning strategy to foster the orderly *reduction* of population, energy use, urban spatial pressures, or tourism.

diffusion   Planned or unplanned spread of cultural patterns from one society and area to another.

diner   1. Restaurant car on a train; 2. Person eating in a restaurant; 3. Small, inexpensive place to eat.

dinghy   Small rowboat. *See also* boat; ship; yacht.

dining program   Package or prearranged set of restaurant meals offered for sale to a client or visitor. Usually commissionable for the agent or seller; usually offers the purchaser some discount.

dinner   English term for the big meal of the day. Now the evening meal but originally the meal taken at midday.

direct flight   Flight that does not require a passenger to change planes, although there may be intermediate stops.

directional tariff   Special reduced fare for one leg of a trip, often contingent upon the season of the year or the purchase of a roundtrip.

direct route   Shortest distance route from one point to another.

disclaimer of liability   Legal concept in which responsibility for error, wrongful action, or omissions is disavowed, as in the case of a travel agent who sells a tour package but disclaims responsibility for problems encountered while on the tour.

disclosure rule   Rule enacted and enforced by the Federal Trade Commission (FTC) mandating franchisers to provide all prospective licensees (franchisees) with detailed financial organizational information before entering into any agreement with them.

Discover America Travel Organizations (DATO)   *See* Travel Industry Association of America.

discretionary time   Time available after necessary work and home tasks are completed. Leisure time.

disembark   To leave a ship or aircraft.

dispersed development strategy   Planned scattering of tourism facilities, to avoid undue pressures on any single area.

disposables   Broad category of items designed to be used only once and then discarded rather than washed or cleaned for reuse. Included are bed sheets, pillow cases, table cloths, napkins, maid uniforms, and fast food containers.

district sales manager (DSM)   Person responsible for administering sales functions at the district office of an airline, steamship line, car rental company, or other large organization with multiple offices.

DIT   *See* domestic independent tour.

docent   Guide; a paid employee or volunteer responsible for providing guided tours of a facility or area.

dome car   Specially designed railway car with a glass roof for sightseeing. Also called a *bubble car.*

domestic airline   Any carrier operating primarily within the boundaries of its own country.

domestic escorted tour (DET)   Packaged, preplanned itinerary within the traveler's home country, including the services of a tour manager/escort.

domestic independent tour (DIT)   Term used in the United States or Canada to describe a prepaid, unescorted itinerary within a country. Also known as *domestic inclusive tour.*

domestic market   Residents of an area, state, or country who use the tourism facilities of that area, or have the potential to use it.

dominant landform   Distinguishing geological formation that serves as the identifying feature of an area, such as Niagara Falls.

doorman   Luxury service offered by some hotels whereby an employee is stationed at the main entrance for the purpose of calling a passing taxi, providing general directions, and opening the doors for guests.

double   1. Hotel or motel room designed to accommodate two persons; 2. Reservation for two persons; 3. Room provided with a double bed.

double-double   Room designed to accommodate two, three, or four persons; a room with two double beds.

double-occupancy rate   Per person room rate contingent upon someone else also occupying the room as a paying customer.

double room rate   Rate for a room to be occupied by two people.

downgrade   To change to a lower-grade class of service.

downline   All segments (legs) of an itinerary after the originating flight.

downtime   Period when employees or equipment are not engaged in revenue-producing activity.

drawing room   *See* railroad classes of service (U.S.A. and Canada).

drifter   Person wishing to travel as inexpensively and spontaneously as possible, seeking close contact with local culture and accepting responsibility for what happens along the way.

dry lease   Rental of a vehicle that includes only the vehicle; no crew, supplies, fuel, or maintenance service is included.

DSM   *See* district sales manager.

dual mode transit   Proposed transportation system that would combine the needs of personal transportation with the benefits of public transport. Vehicles would be suited to both personal use and some variation of moving platform or "automatic pilot" for use when long distances need to be covered.

duplex   Accommodation suite with two floors, connected by a private stairway.

duty, customs   *See* customs duty.

duty-free imports   Government-specified list of item amounts, and item categories that are free of tax or duty charges when brought into the country.

duty-free shop   Business establishment often located within an international terminal, where passengers departing on international trips can purchase goods without imposition of a duty or tax because the items are not received until departure, and thus will not be used in the country where the terminal is located.

E

economic imperialism   In tourism, situations where residents believe that they are no longer in control of their area; that outsiders own the land and facilities, which are in turn used by other outsiders.

economic indicators   General term for any number of data sources used for measuring overall community, regional, or national economic performance.

economy hotel   Hotel with no private bath facilities and limited services. Also referred to as a tourist or second class hotel.

ecosystem   Community together with its habitat; an interacting biological and environmental system.

efficiency unit   Hotel or motel room providing facilities for in-room cooking of meals.

elapsed flying time   Time spent in actual air travel, the amount of time remaining after all scheduled ground time at intermediate stops has been deducted.

elasticity   Economic concept measuring the sensitivity of customer demand to changes in the price of goods and services. Tourism tends to evidence an elastic pattern, that is, sales increase or decrease dramatically when the price of a tourism good or service is lowered or raised only slightly. A nonelastic situation would exist if the change in customer demand equaled the direction and magnitude of the change in price.

elderhostel   Network of several hundred universities and colleges in the United States and Canada that offer persons over sixty years of age the opportunity to experience a combined program of education and adventure. Accommodations are provided in campus dormitories and special courses are offered.

elevated railway   Railway system, usually electric, that runs at least in part on an elevated structure above the street. *See also* subway; train.

embark   To go on board a ship or aircraft.

embarkation card   *See* boarding pass.

empathy   Ability to perceive a situation from another's viewpoint.

English breakfast   Hearty breakfast usually served in Great Britain and Ireland, consisting of cereals, meats, egg dishes, breads, and beverages. *See also* continental breakfast.

enplane   To go on board an aircraft.

entree   Originally, food served between heavy courses. Now generally refers to the main dish in a multicourse meal.

entrepreneur   In developing areas, a resident who begins a business by successfully adapting an idea developed elsewhere, with the effect that employment opportunities and capital are generated.

entry fee   *See* head tax.

entry requirements   Established by national governments, the official documentation necessary to enter a given country, which may include proof of citizenship, passport, visa, vaccination certificate.

entry tax   *See* head tax.

environmental bubble   Tendency of some tourists to prefer "home town" style food, hotels, and companions even while visiting a foreign destination.

EP   *See* European plan.

epicure   Person dedicated to the enjoyment of good food and spirits.

equator   Great circle whose plane is at right angles to the earth's axis, dividing the earth into northern and southern hemispheres. *See also* crossing the line.

escalator   *See* travelator.

escape   Psychological adjustment to conflict by avoiding the frustrating situation. Also, in tourism, the escape from routine life to an idealized situation or experience.

escort   *See* tour manager.

escorted tour   A foreign or domestic tour using the services of a tour manager. *See also* domestic escorted tour; foreign escorted tour; tour manager.

escrow account   Legally required safeguard of funds such as customer deposits and prepayments. Escrow accounts are held in licensed financial institutions for payout when the service has been delivered.

estimated time of arrival (ETA)   Point in time at which a carrier (usually an aircraft) is expected to reach a location or destination; also used to refer to the time a guest or group is expected to arrive at a hotel or other location.

estimated time of departure (ETD)   Point in time at which a carrier (usually an aircraft) is expected to leave a location; also the time at which a guest or group is expected or scheduled to leave a hotel or other location.

ETA   *See* estimated time of arrival.

ETC   *See* European Travel Commission.

ETD   *See* estimated time of departure.

ethnic agency   Travel agency specializing in providing services usually used by a given ethnic group, or one which has a clientele of a specific ethnicity.

ethnic group   Category of people distinguishable by race, religion, national origin, or a combination of these factors.

ethnic travel   Tourism patterns that appeal to specific ethnic groups.

ethnocentrism   Conviction—emotional rather than logical—that one's own group is superior to all others, together with the tendency to judge other groups by one's own group's standards.

Eurailpass   Railroad ticket providing unlimited rail travel throughout 14 countries of Western Europe. Fares are flat rates for specified number of days and are available at special children's rates as well as for adults.

European plan (EP)   Hotel accommodations with no meals included in the price of the room.

European Travel Commission (ETC)   Membership organization of national government and private business representatives that seeks to promote travel to and within Europe.

event   Cultural, artistic, sporting, or other special or unique activity that is organized to attract and be attended by the general public, free of charge or for a fee.

excess baggage ticket   Receipt given by a carrier to a passenger who has paid excess baggage charges.

exchange order   Prepaid service order for transportation, accommodations, or other travel-related services issued by a carrier or a travel agent.

exclusivity   The effect of the Air Traffic Conference decisions that prohibit airlines from paying commission to entities lacking ATC accreditation and ATC standardized ticket stock. As a consequence, travel agents and airlines have exclusivity on the sale of air transportation.

excursion   Short-term roundtrip. Travel experience.

excursionist   Defined by the World Tourism Organization as a temporary visitor staying less than 24 hours in a country.

executive chef   Experienced chef or cook who manages all of the kitchen activities and employees, including menu selection, food purchasing, and personnel decisions.

executive room   Multipurpose hotel room designed for small meetings or sleeping. Usually provided with couches that convert into beds.

exhibition cooking   Specialized attraction; food prepared by experts in a location that permits observation by onlookers.

expatriate   Citizen of one country who resides for an extended period in another country.

explorer   Tourist characterized by an independent itinerary, high acceptance of responsibility for what occurs, and a desire to experience contact with the culture visited.

expressway   *See* highway.

extension   Optional trips, offered at extra cost, that may be taken by members of a tour group before, during, or after a basic tour.

F

FAA   *See* Federal Aviation Administration.

fabricated foods   Food items that have been prepared almost to the final point by a supplier; preparation time is greatly reduced as is the need for skilled restaurant personnel.

Fahrenheit   Measure of temperature where the freezing point of water is 32° and boiling point is 212°. *See also* Celsius.

familiarization trip/tour   Trips or tours offered to travel writers and agency personnel by airlines and other suppliers as a way of informing the customer-influencing segments of the industry. Often called a *fam trip*.

family hotels   Commercial accommodations that specialize in providing the space, services, and atmosphere desired by people traveling with small children.

family plan   Discount offered by hotels, airlines, and resorts to members of a family traveling together.

fam trip/tour   *See* familiarization trip/tour.

fare   Money paid for transportation on an air, ground, or water carrier. There are many different types of fares, especially airline fares. *Normal fares* (first class, coach, economy, etc.) are the standard all-year fares; *off-season fares* are good only at certain times of the year and on certain days; *promotional fares* are lower in cost than normal fares but may carry restrictions and may be valid only on specific days, times, or flights, and may require a minimum stay abroad or at the destination; *night fares* are good only on certain flights departing late at night; *family plan fares* are for family members traveling together; *tour-*

basing fares are reduced fares of an inclusive tour or package tour; *child fares* are for anyone from 2 to 12 years; *infant fares* are for anyone under 2 years of ˌ age; *standby fares* are fares for travelers who wait at the check-in counter for space to become available on a specific flight.

fare construction unit *See* foreign currency unit.

fast food Type of food service. While intended to refer to the speed of service (from ordering to delivery), the term is also applied to the food itself.

fathom Measure of depth; 6 feet.

FCU *See* foreign currency unit.

feasibility study Process by which marketing and financial information is collected, interpreted, and analyzed for the purpose of deciding whether or not to proceed with the project under consideration. A feasibility study allows decisionmakers to consider changes and predict the future profitability of various alternatives.

Federal Aviation Act Federal act that created the Federal Aviation Administration, charged with the regulation, promotion, and development of civil aviation in the United States.

Federal Aviation Administration (FAA) Governmental body under the United States Department of Transportation, which exercises an overall control of airports, equipment, pilots and routes, and issues mandatory requirements and standards to govern civil aviation .

Federal Maritime commission (FMC) United States federal agency charged with the regulation of international steamship, cargo, and passenger services.

feeder airline *See* local service airline.

feeder roads Major roadways or highways that allow for efficient travel to and from the resort vacation area and the customer's point of origin.

ferryboat Vessel used to transport passengers and cars across a river, bay, or other relatively narrow body of water.

ferry mileage Distance in miles an aircraft is flown without passengers to where it must pick up tour members. Airlines charge for these air miles; therefore, the less ferry miles schedules require, the lower the operating cost of the charter.

FET *See* foreign escorted tour.

final itinerary Complete schedule, delivered by the travel agent shortly before actual departure, which spells out in detail the exact program mapped out for the traveler, including flight or train numbers, departure times, and so forth.

firming Act of verifying with a passenger that reservations held will be used.

first class hotel Hotel offering a high standard and variety of services; most rooms have a private bath.

first class service Service established for the carriage of passengers or care of clients at premium fares that are specifically designated. A service above that which is regularly and ordinarily provided. The term is often used as an advertising cliche with no substantive differentiating ability.

FIT *See* foreign independent tour.

FIT operator/wholesaler Company that specializes in creating and operating FITs for travel agents to sell to their clients. *See* foreign independent tour.

five freedoms *See* freedoms of the air.

flagship Newest, largest, or finest ship of a steamship or cruise line.

flag stop Point on a carrier's route that is served only when passengers or goods are to be picked up or discharged.

flat rate Price or rate that is not discounted in consideration of frequency or volume of use.

flight attendant Person responsible for looking after the welfare of the passengers.

flight crew Those responsible for operating an aircraft; includes the pilots, flight engineer, and flight attendants.

flight, deadhead Transporting an aircraft for the purpose of moving or returning it to some location without revenue passengers or cargo. Also called a *ferry flight.*

flight, extra section Additional flight added to an existing schedule during a particularly heavily traveled period.

flight, nonscheduled Flight that is not in accordance with published schedules or timetables.

flight number Specific designation of a flight.

flight, scheduled Any aircraft itinerary that is periodically operated, separately designated by a flight number or otherwise, and listed in the published schedules of an air carrier.

fly-drive package Tour package that includes airline transport from one's point of origin to the destination and return, and the use of an automobile for local transport while at the destination.

flyer Printed advertising, distributed to potential customers by hand or by mail.

FMC *See* Federal Maritime Commission.

folder Printed material folded so as to fit into an envelope or counter rack. Designed to attract attention and provide the reader with the basic facts of a tourism service or destination.

folio Written or electronic record of a guest's account, containing a perpetual balance of the guest's financial transactions within the property.

folk landscape "Natural" folk landscapes are areas interesting to tourists because of unique or beautiful ways of life. "Preserved" or "recreated" folk landscapes are created for tourists; such theme areas bring together, in a community setting, the image-enhancing elements of past and contemporary folk society.

folklore Beliefs, myths, stories, and traditions of the past that survive in the present for a group, community, or society.

folk society Relatively fragile social grouping characterized by a degree of geographical isolation, a strong sense of unity, and a system of informal sanctions.

footpath Pedestrian walkway that may be designed to offer the user a special visual advantage of the area at a level of ease or difficulty appropriate for the user.

foreign currency unit (FCU) Method of basing fares established by IATA to elminate the problems of fluctuating currency values. Also called *fare construction unit*.

foreign escorted tour (FET) Preplanned all-inclusive tour outside the tourist's own country, including the services of a tour manager.

foreign exchange earnings Monies acquired when foreign tourists come into a country. *Net foreign exchange earnings* are a more useful measure; that is, the amount remaining after the costs of imported goods, services and expertise necessary to provide and maintain touristic facilities are subtracted from the monies generated by visiting foreign tourists.

foreign exchange rate Rate at which the money of one country can be exchanged for the money of another country.

foreign flag airline Any air carrier other than a United States air carrier engaged in international air transportation. Also means a non-United States air carrier operating within the boundaries of its own country.

foreign independent tour (FIT) International prepaid trip with the itinerary planned to the traveler's specifications.

forest preserve *See* preserve.

Fourth World Cultural groups throughout the world who are now officially part of some official nation not of their own making. Existing as separate cultures within a larger society, Fourth World people have the potential of benefiting, or being exploited, as a touristic resource. Their unique ways of life, artifacts, and rituals are sought by visitors to the area.

FP *See* full pension.

franchising Practice of selling or leasing to an individual or group the right to use the franchiser's name, products, or services, usually for a percentage of gross sales in addition to a one-time fee.

freedoms of the air Basic traffic rights, as bilaterally arranged between nations. Freedoms of commercial airlines include 1. the right to overfly; 2. the right to land for technical reasons; 3. the right to carry from home country to another country; 4. the right to carry from another country to home country; and 5. the right to carry between foreign countries. Also called "the five freedoms."

free pass Ticket or some other authorized admission obtained without payment of the stated fee.

free port 1. Port or part of a port where cargo can be unloaded and goods deposited without payment of customs duty; 2. A port open under equal terms to all vessels.

freeway *See* highway.

freighter travel Passenger-carrying freighters are vessels principally engaged in transportation of goods and licensed to carry up to twelve passengers; similar vessels that are licensed to carry more than twelve passengers are often called cargoliners.

French service Style of restaurant service; each food item is individually served to the guest at the table, as opposed to preparing the guest's plate in the kitchen.

front desk Area in the main lobby of a commercial accommodation where the guest checks in. The front desk also provides key storage, mail distribution, and information.

front office Functional area in a hotel, motel, or other facility which is responsible for coordinating all guest/customer services including registration, providing information, maintaining guest accounts, and settling the final bill.

front office manager Person responsible for all front office functions of a hotel or motel, including check-in, room reservations, accounting, and so forth.

front of the house Industry term for those portions of the hotel, motel, restaurant, or other facility that the customer comes directly in contact with under normal conditions. *See* back of the house.

fuel stop Point on an air carrier's route scheduled to refuel the aircraft but not to enplane or deplane passengers or cargo.

full pension (FP) Term used in Europe to denote a hotel rate including three meals per day. *See* American plan.

fully appointed Description of a travel agency that has been officially appointed by the major airlines, steamship, and cruise conferences to sell products and services and issue tickets.

fun morality Attitude that enjoyment is the real purpose of life: "If it feels good, it is good."

G

galley Area of a ship or aircraft where food is prepared.

gangway Passageway or ramp to a ship for embarking and disembarking passengers. *See also* jetway; ramp.

gap In reference to an airline itinerary, a portion or leg of the trip traveled by means other than an IATA or ATC airline. Also may be shown as *surface* on the flight coupon.

garni *See* hotel garni.

gateway city   City that functions as the first destination for visitors to the area, due to location and transportation patterns.

gear   Slang for the numerous items of equipment deemed necessary for an activity, such as camping, fishing, or photography.

GEM   *See* ground effect machine.

GIT   *See* group inclusive tour.

give-away   Novelty or premium distributed by a business as an attention getter, or as an inducement to purchase something else.

go foreign   To sail on a vessel bound for foreign countries.

golden ghetto   Concentration of tourists who are noticeably of a different color or different standard of living (wealthier) than residents of the area.

go-show   Traveler waiting to take the place of a confirmed reservation holder who does not appear. The traveler has no reservation and thus is not entitled to compensation if the desired flight is missed.

gourmet   One who appreciates fine food and drink, an orientation toward food preparation which stresses the finest of ingredients and attention to detail.

grand tour   Itinerary of extended duration or relative luxury.

gratuity   Tip. Optional, variable payment by a customer for services, over and above the charge for a meal, room, or other purchase. *See also* service charge.

graveyard shift   Night shift at a hotel or any other place of employment; usually 11 P.M. to 7 A.M.

great circle route   Shortest distance between two points; navigation of an aircraft on a great circle of the earth.

greenbelt   Strip of vacant or agricultural land encircling a community and serving as a buffer between urban use areas; often community owned and the result of deliberate destination area planning.

Greenwich mean time   Solar (standard) time at Greenwich, England (a suburb of London, located on the prime meridian, 0°) from which standard time for most of the world is calculated. *See also* mean time.

gross national product (GNP)   Comprehensive measure of a nation's total production, based upon the market value of goods and services produced during some time period, usually a month or a year.

gross register ton   Indication of the size of a passenger ship; 100 cubic feet of enclosed space.

ground arrangements   Land services provided to a client at each destination visited in an itinerary. May include transfer to a hotel, car rental, entertainment tickets, and so forth.

ground effect machine (GEM)   Aircraft or vessel that "rides" on a cushion of air that exists between it and the land or water surface. The hovercraft is one example increasingly used in tourism, as it is capable of operating above shallow and deep water, swamps, and solid land.

ground operator Company that provides local transportation, sightseeing, and other services to a client at a destination. *See also* contractor.

ground time 1. Time spent on the ground at intermediate stops; 2. The time spent in airports and waiting for connecting flights.

group inclusive tour (GIT) Prepaid tour, allowing special air fares to a group and requiring that all the members must travel on the same flight round trip, and must travel together during their entire time abroad.

group planner Printed brochure or packet of materials for use by agents, organizations, and individuals interested in planning travel experiences for groups of people. Special services, available only for groups, are highlighted as well as prices, options, and persons to contact for additional information.

guaranteed reservation Advance booking, with payment guaranteed even if the guest does not arrive, unless cancelled in accordance with the accommodation's cancellation policy.

guaranteed tour Tour guaranteed to operate as shown in the brochure regardless of the number of participants booked, unless cancelled by the tour operator by a certain date.

guest Customer of a hotel, motel, or restaurant.

guest cycle Sequenced pattern of activities followed by a guest or customer, such as arrival, occupancy, departure; or presale, point of sale, and postsale.

guest file *See* guest history card.

guest folio *See* folio.

guest history card Composite record of the several registrations of a repeat guest, showing the frequency of visits, the rooms occupied, length of stay, and any relevant special information or requests.

guest house *See* tourist home.

guest-night One night spent by one guest in a hotel, motel, or other accommodation.

guide Someone who is licensed and employed to take tourists on local sightseeing excursions.

guidebook Multipage listing of accommodations, routes, places of interest, restaurants, history, and other information for a region, destination area, state, or country. Also called a *travel directory*.

guided tour Escorted sightseeing trip.

H

half pension Hotel rate including bed, breakfast, and one other meal. Also called *demi pension*, or *modified American plan*.

hall   Large room for meetings or banquets, as in the case of a convention hall.

handicrafts   Product and the process by which small items of high manual skill, low capital investment, and low technology are made. Often made of local materials in a style or theme of local heritage by the residents of an area for sale to tourists.

hand luggage   *See* baggage.

head   The toilet aboard ship.

head tax   Fee collected by a city or national government for entry into or departure from that city or country.

health resort   Complex of facilities and natural features used by tourists interested in health-giving qualities, such as mineral waters, sun, air, exercise, and expert health personnel. Also called a *spa*.

health spa   *See* health resort.

hedonism   Philosophy of pleasure, nonwork, and enjoyment; consumption for the sake of consumption.

helicopter   *See* aircraft.

heliport   Landing and take-off area for helicopters. May be located on the tops of tall urban buildings and at transportation terminals, thus providing a fast air taxi service between the areas.

heritage   Unique historical and cultural accomplishments of an area and its people as remembered or preserved for present and future generations to experience.

high risk   Guest with an accumulated total of as-yet unpaid charges that approaches, equals, or exceeds the house limit.

high season   Time of year at any destination when tourist traffic and (usually) rates are highest. *See also* peak use period.

highway   Roadway for use by automobiles, trucks, and some other vehicles that offers relatively safe, unhampered, efficient, and fast travel because it has been designed to be as straight and level as possible with few or no stops. Often designed as a multilane divided highway, that is, having an open space between the directional lanes. The interstate highway system was a federally funded project which linked virtually every part of the United States; variously known as an *expressway* or a *freeway;* a *tollway* or *turnpike* is identical, except that a fee is charged for its use.

highway patrol   Branch of law enforcement that monitors the roadways of an area.

highway signing legislation   Series of existing and pending federal, state, and local laws aimed at influencing the number, size, type, and location of informational signs along roadways. Roadway users are central to the dilemma in that while they appreciate natural uncluttered beauty, they also need information as to attractions, fuel stations, restaurants, and accommodations.

hijacking   *See* aircraft piracy.

hire car   British and European term for a rented car.

hitch-hiking   Form of travel in which a person signals a request for a ride from passing vehicles traveling in the desired direction. Popular as a low expense youth-oriented form of transport, although illegal in many areas.

holiday   Day established by law or custom on which ordinary work is suspended; outside the United States of America, a vacation or time away from work.

holiday ghetto   Area designed to isolate tourists from local culture.

holiday village   Complex of multiple accommodation units grouped around a central core of food and recreational facilities. A self-sustaining resort in the sense that everything needed or desired is available within the complex.

honeymoon package   Preplanned itinerary designed for newlyweds, usually featuring numerous in-room luxuries.

horizontal elevator   Any of a number of existing and proposed people-movers, as in the case of the monorails and shuttle vehicles now used at airports and major amusement parks.

hospitality industry   Used interchangeably with *tourism* and *tourism industry* but focusing attention on the responsibility of industry personnel to be hospitable hosts and managers of what takes place. *See* tourism.

hospitality suite   Hotel or motel room used for hospitality or entertainment, rather than sleeping, usually at a convention or meeting.

host   Employees of a property or destination area, to the extent that they treat their tourist-customer as a guest, that is, someone in need of and deserving of specialized attention, services, and consideration.

host community   The term refers to the permanent residents of a tourism destination area; the residents of a town, area, or nation who are influenced by the presence of tourists and who serve officially or accidentally as hosts of the tourist by sharing their land, facilities, highways, and culture with them.

hostel   Accommodations often for specific groups of users, such as youth, club members, and so forth, where the facilities are shared, inexpensive, supervised, and basic.

hostelry   General, somewhat literary term for any place providing food, lodging, or both for travelers. *See* hostel.

hotel   Places offering sleeping accommodations for hire to travelers and transients. Generally the term is synonymous with *inn, motel, motor hotel,* or *motor lodge.* The differences between these related forms of accommodation are a matter of degree. Hotels are generally larger in size, with numerous services for guests who may stay for several days. *See also* motel; motor hotel; motor lodge.

hotel capacity   Number of rooms available for sale, or the number of people who can comfortably (and legally) be accommodated in a given property or destination area.

hotel chain Two or more hotel properties owned or managed by the same company, independent of the customers' awareness or company advertising of that fact.

hotel classifications No common worldwide rating system exists for hotels; the star rating system used in many European countries comes closest. Under the star rating system a five star hotel would be the very best and a one star a budget or economy establishment. Some rating systems may have subdivided classifications. For example, a hotel designated as *super deluxe* and one designated as *luxurious* may both fall within the deluxe category; there may also be *upper first class* and *lower first class*. An unofficial rating system might run as follows: *Deluxe:* the very best top-grade hotel, all rooms with private baths, high quality furniture, carpeting, and accessories, many public rooms and services, and a high standard of service. *First class:* Medium priced, most rooms with private bath, well furnished, adequate public rooms, and good service. *Second class* or *tourist:* Low-cost hotel, some hotels might have rooms with private bath, no-frill services. *Third class, budget,* or *economy:* Few if any rooms with private bath, limited services such as no dining rooms or breakfast only.

hotel garni Usually a smaller, commercial property providing accommodations without meal facilities, or providing breakfast only. Also called *aparthotel.*

hotelier Hotel keeper, owner, or manager.

hotel industry Accommodation segment of tourism, including primarily hotels and motels. The term stresses the fact that such businesses, while often individually owned and small, warrant recognition as an industry when viewed as a total.

hotel package Combination of services often including transportation, transfers, rooms, and use of all facilities.

hotel register Permanent record of all guests; each guest is required by law to sign in upon arrival.

hotel representative Person or company retained by one or more hotels to arrange hotel reservations for wholesalers, travel agents, and the public. Often simply referred to as a hotel "rep."

Hotel and Restaurant Employee and Bartenders International Union (HREBIU) Trade union representing employees of the hospitality industry.

hotel voucher Coupon issued by a tour operator to cover payment for all specified prepaid tour features. Guests surrender the hotel voucher on check-in and the hotel sends the voucher and billing statement to the tour operator for payment.

hot line One or more telephone numbers provided and advertised to provide fast, accurate information, to make reservations, or to handle complaints. In most cases the number is intended for some specific use and user, such as retail travel agents, customers with problems, or for providing information on gasoline availability.

houseboat   Powered floating watercraft that includes an enclosed living area.

House Congressional Tourism Caucus   Group of members of the United States House of Representatives established as a means of obtaining support for tourism. *See also* Senate Tourism Caucus.

house exchange   Practice of trading use of one's home for the use of another's, in a different locality. Often arranged by an agency, which may also be called a *house exchange.*

house flag   Official flag of a steamship company.

housekeeping   Nonrevenue operating department responsible for preparing and maintaining the guest rooms and public areas of a hotel, motel, or other commercial facility.

housekeeping cottage   Freestanding accommodation unit, which includes all necessary cooking equipment and bedding for guests. Employees complete a major cleanup between guests, but the guests are responsible for all such work during their stay. *See also* individual housing.

house limit   Amount of the total charges a property allows a guest to incur before partial or full payment is required. Also known as line of credit.

housing bureau   Information center, often government-sponsored, established to arrange and coordinate accommodations for large meetings, conventions, and other major events.

hovercraft   *See* ground effect machine.

HREBIU   *See* Hotel and Restaurant Employees and Bartenders International Union.

HRI school   Educational institution or program offering post-secondary school courses in hotel, restaurant, institutional, or tourism education.

hydrofoil   Water transport vessel using fins or foils to raise the craft partly out of the water at high speeds, thus reducing friction.

I

IAAPA   *See* International Association of Amusement Parks and Attractions.

IACA   *See* International Air Charter Association

IACVB   *See* International Association of Conventions and Visitor Bureaus.

IAFE   *See* International Association of Fairs and Expositions.

IAMAT   *See* International Association for Medical Assistance to Travelers.

IATA   *See* International Air Transport Association.

IATC   *See* Inter American Travel Congress.

IATM   *See* International Association of Tour Managers.

ICAO   *See* International Civil Aviation Organization.

ICC   *See* Interstate Commerce Commission.

ICCA   *See* International Congress and Convention Association.

ICMOS   *See* International Council for Monuments and Sites.

ICTA   *See* Institute of Certified Travel Agents.

IFSEA   *See* International Food Service Executives Association.

IHA   *See* International Hotel Association.

image   Mental picture or set of expectations about a person, place, or activity that exists (voluntarily or through suggestions) before the actual experience.

impact   Envisioned or actual consequences—negative or positive—of a decision. The impact may be economic, sociocultural, political, environmental, or other; direct or indirect; intended or not; favorable or unfavorable. *See* multiplier effect.

impulse travel   Travel characterized by relatively little preplanning, or a deviation from what was originally planned; a decision based on freedom of chice and mobility.

inaugural   Initial use of a new route or a new type of aircraft or other vehicle. Often the occasion of promotional festivities, including free passage for travel agents and travel writers.

incentive commission   *See* override.

incentive fare   Discounted airline fare for incentive groups. *See* incentive travel.

incentive travel   Practice of rewarding a successful salesperson or department personnel with a bonus in the form of expense-paid travel. Incentive travel programs are prepared by various segments of the travel industry and offered as a way for any type of business to promote sales and reward employees at the same time.

inclusive tour   Tour including many tour components such as air fare, hotels, and sightseeing. *See also* IT number.

income differential   In tourism, the difference between the standard of living of residents of an area as compared to visitors.

income elasticity   Economic concept. *Low* income elasticity describes a condition where purchases of a given product or service will change very little whether incomes rise or fall. Such products or services are usually considered necessities. Luxuries, such as travel, are usually perceived as related to *high* income elasticity.

income, net tourism   Amount calculated by deducting all direct and indirect leakages from the total amount spent by tourists in a specific area.

independent   Both the owner and the property owned where only one business establishment exists. Small chains are sometimes called independent chains, especially when they compete with larger chains.

indirect air carrier   Person, tour operator, or travel agent who buys charter space from an airline for the express purpose of reselling it to the public, usually as part of a tour package.

individual housing   The term covers a wide variety of free-standing accommodations, including cottages, chalets, and villas. Some units may be part of a hotel or resort complex and include maid service and other amenities in the price. Owner-occupied second homes and vacation homes are also regarded as examples of individual housing.

inflight feeding   Provision of food and beverages for passengers on board an aircraft. Generally involves an efficient high volume flight-catering kitchen located at an airport; the food is prepared and packaged there, with final preparations made in flight.

information center   *See* travel information centers.

infrastructure   Such investments as utilities (water, sewer, electricity), transport (roads, harbors, airports), site development, health care, schools.

in-house agency   *See* in-plant agency.

inn   *See* hotel.

innkeeper   Tourism accommodation manager of an inn, hotel, or motel.

innkeepers' lien   Legal right of an innkeeper to keep the property of a guest for unpaid charges.

in-plant agency   Travel agency, or travel agency branch, located on a company's premises handling the business needs of the company.

inside selling   Strategy that seeks to sell additional goods and services to persons who are already customers of some of a business' offerings. For example, the guest of a hotel may be invited to use the hotel's barber shop; a restaurant patron may welcome the suggestion of having wine with the meal. Also called *in-house selling.*

Institute of Certified Travel Agents (ICTA)   Industry organization offering a voluntary education accreditation program for retail travel agents.

Inter American Travel Congress (IATC)   Annual professional meeting concerned with the development of travel and tourism in the western hemisphere. Associated with the Organization of American States (OAS).

interline   1. Airline employee traveling on another airline; 2. Airline reservationist who makes reservations for passengers on other carriers.

interline representative   Salesperson or account executive who calls on other airlines.

intermodal   Use of more than one form or mode of transportation. Example: airline to destination; rented car at the destination.

International Air Charter Association (IACA) Trade association of supplemental and charter airlines.

International Air Transport Association (IATA) Worldwide trade association of international airlines. The IATA conference promotes a unified system of air transportation on international routes; sets fares and rates, safety standards, conditions of service; and appoints and regulates travel agents to sell international tickets.

International Association of Amusement Parks and Attractions (IAAPA) Trade association.

International Association of Conventions and Visitor Bureaus (IACVB) Trade association.

International Association of Fairs and Expositions (IAFE) Trade association.

International Association for Medical Assistance to Travelers (IAMAT) Worldwide nonprofit membership association concerned with the health dangers associated with travel and the dissemination of information to reduce such dangers.

International Association of Scientific Experts in Tourism (AIEST) Europe-based world wide association of scientists, educators and government officials interested in tourism; the Association internationale d'experts scientifiques du tourisme (AIEST).

International Association of Tour Managers (IATM) Professional organizational of tour escorts.

International Certificate of Vaccination Document issued by the tourist's local public health service, as approved by the World Health Organization of the United Nations. A record of all required and suggested inoculations and booster shots.

International Civil Aviation Organization (ICAO) Specialized agency of the United Nations, cooperating to develop and standardize aircraft equipment, training, and planning.

International Congress and Convention Association (ICCA) European trade association.

International Council for Monuments and Sites (ICMOS) Organization concerned with the identification, classification, renovation, and protection of monuments and sites of historic significance.

international date line Imaginary line drawn north and south through the Pacific Ocean, largely along the 180th meridian, where, by international agreement, the earth's day begins at midnight, so that when it is Sunday west of the line it is Saturday east of it. Eastbound passengers gain a day when crossing the line; westbound passengers lose a day.

International Food Service Executives Association (IFSEA) Industry organization dedicated to lifelong education and professionalism.

International Health Certificate *See* International Certificate of Vaccination.

International Hotel Association (IHA) Trade association of European hotels.

International Institute for the Unification of Private Law Concerned with national legislation, specifically as it applies to hotels and guests, in an effort to determine a common body of law that is acceptable to all countries.

International Passenger Ship Association (IPSA) Trade association of companies that operate cruises marketed in North America. Supersedes the Trans-Atlantic Passenger Steamship Conference (TAPSC).

International Sightseeing and Tours Association (ISTA) Association of sightseeing tour operators.

International Society of Hotel Association Executives (ISHAE) Trade organization.

international tourist receipts Statistical computation, by country, of the total amount of money spent by foreign tourists when visiting that country.

International Union of Former Hotel School Students (IUFHSS) Group concerned with the global impact of issues confronting the foodservice and hospitality industries.

International Union of Official Travel Organizations *See* World Tourism Organization.

International Union of Railways (UIC) Organized in France, the UIC's (Union Internationale des Chemins de Fers) aim is to improve international rail service.

Interpol Abbreviation of the name of the International Criminal Police Organization, an organization of police forces from over 100 countries. Members agree on mutual help for police problems.

interstate carrier Airline or other transportation company providing service between one state and one or more other states of the United States.

Interstate Commerce Commission (ICC) Federal agency responsible for regulating bus and motorcoach operations and other forms of interstate commerce.

intraline Of or relating to a single carrier.

in transit visitor Person who stops for a short time, out of necessity or because of a short-term attraction, en route to some other location. Also called a *nonstaying visitor.*

intrastate carrier Airline or other transportation company providing service solely within one state of the United States.

investment, foreign Funding or purchase of property by a person or group not citizens of the country affected. Often controversial. *See also* investment, outside.

investment, outside 1. Similar to foreign investment, with the exception that citizenship is not involved; the investors are from outside a community; 2. Funding for a project obtained from sources other than those who will manage and retain majority ownership of the enterprise.

invisible exports/imports Money spent by citizens of a specific country when visiting a foreign destination, or money spent by foreign visitors *to* a given destination.

IPSA *See* International Passenger Ship Association.

ISHAE *See* International Society of Hotel Association Executives.

ISTA *See* International Sightseeing and Tours Association.

itinerary Plan of a journey; a travel route.

itinerary, domestic Travel within the national borders of a country is considered domestic travel; a *domestic itinerary* is made up of such travel. Itineraries within the fifty united states are considered domestic.

itinerary, international/territorial Using the United States as a base, itineraries between a point in the fifty united states and a point outside of these states; between points outside of the fifty united states; between the fifty states and a United States possession, or between or within United States possessions.

IT number Code number identifying a tour that has been submitted and approved by the ATC or IATA, and that allows travel agents to obtain override commissions for air transportation sold as part of such approved tours.

IUFHSS *See* International Union of Former Hotel School Students.

IUOTO *See* World Tourism Organization.

J

jet lag Physical condition brought about by the disruption of a person's "body clock"; the change in routine that accompanies long distance travel and tends to result in any of a variety of symptoms, including sleeplessness and short temper. *See also* circadian rhythms.

jetliner Jet propelled passenger aircraft. *See also* aircraft.

jetport *See* airport.

jet set Group of wealthy, notorious, or elite persons considered (primarily by the media) to be trendsetters in fashion, including travel.

jet stream 1. High-velocity wind moving around the earth from west to east at high altitudes; 2. Exhaust stream of a jet aircraft.

jetway Covered passageway leading directly from the airport boarding area to the aircraft. *See also* gangway; ramp.

jitney Usually a private owner-operated car or van, following a flexible route. Passengers are picked up anywhere en route, pay a fee, and share available space as on a bus.

job sharing   Arrangement in which two people assume responsibility for one full-time position. Salary and benefits are often prorated according to the hours each one works.

jumbo jet   Common term for any of a number of wide-bodied aircraft, capable of carrying 300 or more passengers. *See also* aircraft.

junior suite   Large hotel room with the bedroom and sitting area separated by a partition rather than a complete wall.

junket   Ostensibly a business trip, in reality a pleasure trip, often taken at public expense.

junk art   *See* airport art.

junk food   Meals or snacks which, because of ingredients and processing, are relatively high in calories while low in nutritional value. Often used synonymously with *fast food.*

K

keep alone if possible   Steamship or cruise booking in which a passenger traveling alone is willing to share a cabin to avoid paying the single rate but prefers single occupancy. The initials "KIP" on the reservation request alerts the berthing department to try to assign a cabin where the passenger is the only occupant.

kilometer   Unit of distance equal to 3,280 feet, or 5/8 of a statute mile.

KIP   *See* keep alone if possible.

km   *See* kilometer.

knot   Measure of speed equivalent to one nautical mile per hour. *See also* air mile; nautical mile; statute mile.

L

labor intensive   Business or industry requiring more workers (usually unskilled) than capital investment or technology. Traditional agriculture and tourism are among some labor intensive industries.

lanai   Room with a veranda, balcony, or patio.

land arrangements   *See* ground arrangements.

landmark   Prominent manmade or natural feature of an area or community that can serve as a distinguishing entity for what otherwise would be an average area or community.

land only   Provision in a travel brochure that the price stated includes only services to be provided once the client arrives on the scene. Costs of transportation to and from the location where the itinerary starts are not included.

land operator   *See* contractor.

land use planning   Decisions as to what uses will be made of a particular location; such decisions must account for differing and often competing uses, such as strip mining and tourism.

late cancellation   Cancellation of a flight, a room, or some other reserved-space activity or service, after the designated time limit. Although the business establishment would rather have a cancellation late than not at all the customer may be charged some amount, especially if the cancelled space cannot be resold.

latent demand   Estimate or prediction of the number of customers a proposed facility, attraction, or service would attract if it existed. *See* current demand.

late-show   Passenger or customer holding a reservation who arrives at the check-in desk after the designated time.

Latin American Civil Aviation Commission (LICAC)   Regional commission of the International Civil Aviation Organization (ICAO) with the purpose of coordinating air transportation between the member Latin American states.

latitude   Angular distance north or south of the equator, measured in degrees, minutes, and seconds. One minute of latitude is equal to one nautical mile. *See also* longitude; nautical mile.

layout   The arrangement of the various components or elements within an advertisement, a brochure, or a menu.

layover   *See* stopover.

league   Measure of distance that varies in different countries. The American and English land league is three statute miles; the nautical league is three nautical miles.

leakage   Decrease in real foreign exchange earnings caused by the need for importing goods, services, or credit. May be applied to states, regions, or communities, as well as nations.

leg   *See* segment.

leisure industry   Broad spectrum of businesses providing products and services used by persons during their leisure time; tourism is sometimes considered a part of this industry.

leisure phobia   Inability to enjoy one's self while on vacation or during any activity away from work; restlessness and a feeling of wasting time are common symptoms as is a desire to do and see everything while at a destination, in effect approaching the leisure situation as though it were a form of work.

leisure time   *See* discretionary time.

letter of credit   Written document issued by a banking institution, which allows the person named to withdraw money up to a specified amount. Used prior to and as a supplement to credit cards and in international business travel.

LICAC   *See* Latin American Civil Aviation Commission.

licensing   Process by which an agency of government or other regulatory group grants specific permission to persons or businesses to engage in the activity specified by the license. Permission is granted only after certain predetermined qualifications have been met.

lido deck   Area around the swimming pool as well as the deck of a ship on which the swimming pool is located.

life-seeing   Activity/orientation of the tourist who desires to observe and meet the residents of the destination to experience how they live.

lift   Another word for elevator, used in Europe.

limousine   1. Any large, luxurious chauffeur-driven automobile used to transport guests between hotels and transportation terminals, or hired by travelers for sightseeing; 2. A bus used to carry passengers between hotels and transportation terminals.

liner   Large, ocean-going passenger vessel or ship, which is subject to maritime regulations.

linkage   1. Concept that psychological connections may exist between persons and places; for example, a tourist of a specific ethnic background and the nation providing that background; 2. Recognition of the necessity for planning transportation networks in tourist development.

living history attraction   Carefully researched reproduction of a particular historical era, reconstructed with modern sanitation and safety systems. May include "authentic" craftspeople and visitor participation activities.

load factor   Percentage of carrier capacity sold of the total capacity available for sale. If there are 80 paying passengers on a 100-seat aircraft, the load factor is 80%. The *break-even passenger load factor* is the number of paying passengers necessary to obtain sufficient revenue to offset operating expenses. *Revenue passenger load factor* is the proportion of seating capacity actually sold and used, thus generating revenue.

local operator   *See* contractor.

locals   Somewhat insulting term for the residents of an area.

local service airline   Scheduled carrier serving a specific region. Also called a *regional carrier* or a *feeder airline*.

location analysis   Process of selecting a business site in a resort complex among several choices. More detailed and on a smaller scale than planning.

lodging industry   For all practical purposes, identical to the hotel industry, but with broader parameters that include resorts, motels, condominiums, guest houses, and all other forms of commercial accommodations.

log   Official daily record of a ship's proceedings.

longitude   Distance east or west of the meridian of Greenwich, measured in degrees, minutes, and seconds. *See also* Greenwich mean time; latitude.

lounge   Seating area that permits face-to-face conversation with other guests or passengers; also used to identify a relatively smaller entertainment and liquor service, be it free-standing or part of a hotel or restaurant.

lower berth   *See* berth.

low season   Time of year at any destination when tourist traffic and (usually) rates are lowest.

luggage   *See* baggage.

lure book   Multipage promotional material designed to attract tourists into a given area, state, or country. Often government or association sponsored.

M

MAA   *See* Motel Association of America.

maisonette   *See* individual housing.

maitre d'hotel   Head waiter in a restaurant.

management contract   Business agreement that provides the owners of a facility, be it a hotel, restaurant, convention center, or resort complex, with the management expertise to develop/operate their property efficiently. The management firm handles the property for a set percentage of the profit and is generally not involved with the actual ownership.

manifest   Final official listing of all passengers and/or cargo aboard a transportation vehicle or vessel.

manual   Reference book, in tourism, containing detailed schedules, tariffs, rates, designations of service provided by hotels, carriers, or other suppliers.

MAP   *See* modified American Plan.

marina   Commercial or publicly provided sea or fresh water port especially designed to accommodate small privately owned pleasure use motor and sail boats. Small charter boats and other commercial services are often available.

Maritime Administration   Agency of the U.S. Commerce Department with authority over U.S. inland waterways and the transport on them.

market   Portion of a population considered sufficiently homogeneous by reason of race, age, or income, to be appealed to as a separate entity (as college students, senior citizens, and so forth). A *mass market* is one where products and services are developed to appeal to the widest possible range of potential customers. This term is also used in a derogatory sense, of those who purchase such standardized products and services. *Market segments* are those portions of a population more likely to buy a specific product; such portions are the target of specialized promotions and advertising campaigns.

marketing Process of selling goods or services. *Cooperative marketing* is the strategy of pooling funds from different businesses to create a major impact on the market—for example, the use by clothing stores, travel agencies, and airlines of a particular "theme" all at the same time. *Mass marketing* is a strategy of product development and pricing that bases its success on high volume, meaning wide appeal of both products and prices, as well as varied and intense advertising.

market share Percentage of customer sales obtained by a business from an envisioned, often statistically defined single market, or type of customer—be it singles, repeat customers, first time visitors, middle income families, senior citizens, and so forth.

markup Difference between the net rate charged by a tour operator, hotel, or other supplier, and the retail selling price of the service. Generally a percentage of the net rate rather than a fixed amount.

mass society Condition of contemporary urban populations characterized by high mobility, high specialization, and impersonal relationships.

mass tourism Contemporary tendency to create mass demand for specific locations or experiences, as well as the accommodations and transportation to serve such demand.

mass tourist A qualitative rather than quantitative term referring to the type of tourist who is least adventuresome, preferring the familiar in all that is experienced while traveling.

master plan Part of the planning process whereby some agreed-upon future conditions or facilities are achieved step by step. Projected or desired future demand is coupled with a phased program of legal, physical, and social changes that must be realized.

MCO *See* Miscellaneous Charges Order.

mean time Standard time of a particular meridian, measured by the hour angle of the mean sun.

meat breakfast *See* English breakfast.

medical evacuation Emergency transport of a seriously ill guest or tourist to the medical facilities of his choice—usually his home country.

meeting room Room available as a service or for a charge wherein groups may meet with or without meals.

me-generation Media phrase for a contemporary tendency to consider self-fulfillment as one's primary consideration.

menu List of prepared food items available in a restaurant. A *limited menu* offers relatively few basic items, although the variations available may appear to be quite extensive. A *set menu* is selected by someone other than the diner, offering few, if any, choices. Set menus are common at banquets and on tours.

menu board Method of displaying a restaurant's menu outside the entrance.

meridians Great circles passing around the poles at right angles to the equator.

midnight sun Sun as visible at midnight during the summer of arctic and antarctic regions.

milk run Slang expression referring to any commercial transport schedule which includes many stops, thus increasing the time in transit for the passenger. Especially applicable to some early morning railroad schedules in the U.S.

mini bus Small-bus passenger service that uses regular bus stops, usually within an urban or tourism destination area.

minidestination area Location with touristic facilities and activities sufficient to "hold" the tourist for some period of time before continuing on to some other minidestination or destination area. A stop along the way to somewhere else.

minimum connecting time Officially specified minimum amount of time that should exist between a passenger's scheduled connecting flights.

minimum land package Minimum tour, in cost and components, needed to qualify a passenger for an airline inclusive tour, or some other discount fare.

Miscellaneous Charges Order (MCO) A form issued by a travel agent or airline to cover ground arrangements such as sightseeing, hotels, transfers, meals, bus or train transportation, or other services.

missionary complex Derogatory description of the tendency of both business people and tourists to intentionally or unintentionally attempt to change the ways of living or thinking of residents of another country.

mobile home Structure equipped with all of the facilities of a home, which can be moved to a more or less permanent location with relative ease.

modified American plan (MAP) Hotel accommodations including breakfast and either lunch or dinner in the price of the room. Same as demi pension and half pension.

modular Description of a design approach that stresses ease of storage, replacement, or arrangement. May refer to furniture or building parts.

mom and pop business Small business owned and operated by a husband and wife or family.

motel Commercial accommodations usually located along a roadway or expressway for use by people traveling by automobile. Facilities are often limited as guests tend to arrive late in the afternoon and leave early the next morning. *See also* hotel; motor hotel.

Motel Association of America (MAA) National organization of motel operator state associations in the U.S.

motel industry Collective term for those who make a living owning and operating motels, and the properties involved.

motivation Explanation of why persons do or don't do something; the causes are called drives, motives, needs, values, instincts, depending on the theory being used; some causes for behavior are thought to be unconscious. Tourism in its various forms is the result of motivation, that is, individuals are somehow motivated to seek satisfaction in touristic activities and experiences.

motivational climate Factors and influences in a work environment or at a destination that affect the achievement of personal or business goals.

motorcoach Bus designed to carry passengers in comfort; often includes a bathroom, reclining seats, music, and air conditioning.

motorcoach tour Tour itinerary using a chartered bus as the means of transportation to each scheduled destination.

motor home Self-contained, self-propelled mobile unit containing all the necessities of home—bathroom, kitchen, beds, airconditioning, water supply, electrical generator, etc.; sometimes selected as an alternative to the motel or hotel because it offers a new dimension of travel freedom. The units can be purhased or rented.

motor hotel Similar to a motel; often offering more deluxe facilities. *See* motel.

motoring Travel by automobile for the primary purpose of enjoyment.

motor lodge Similar to a motel but offering more services and facilities. *See* motel.

mountain resort Commercial multiactivity or service tourism facility located in a mountain setting. *See also* resort.

moving sidewalk *See* travelator.

MTS Motor Turbine Ship.

multilevel zoning Designation of uses vertically as well as horizontally, as in the case of an area where underground parking facilities, street-level commercial shops, mid-level office space, and top-level hotel facilities are permitted for the same land area.

multinationals Business organizations that own or control companies or operations in several countries.

multiplier effect Concept that tourist expenditures in an area generate more expenditures, and thus more money, as the tourist income is spent by residents who receive it as wages or profits. The multiplier effect can be estimated statistically.

multipurpose use Design approach whereby a facility is able to provide for more than one group or kind of activity.

mutual aid pact Agreement between airlines to allocate, to a member airline affected by a strike, a portion of the increased revenue earned by the remaining member airlines not affected by the strike.

MV Motor Vessel.

N

NAC *See* National Air Carrier Association.

NAMBO   *See* National Association of Motor Bus Owners.

NATA   *See* National Air Transportation Association.

NATC   *See* National Air Transport Conference.

National Air Carrier Association (NACA)   Trade association representing supplemental and charter airlines.

National Air Transportation Association (NATA)   Trade association representing commuter, air taxi, small cargo-, and mail-carrying airlines.

National Air Transport Conference (NATC)   Trade association of United States commuter and scheduled air taxi airlines.

National Association of Motor Bus Owners (NAMBO)   Association of intercity and charter bus companies.

National Association of Travel Organizations (NATO)   Trade association headquartered in Washington, D.C.

National Institute for the Foodservice Industry (NIFI)   Trade organization concerned with the continuing education of foodservice employees.

national park   Area designated by the federal government for public education and enjoyment. In some cases, such areas must be limited in access to preserve their unique qualities. Areas so designated are unique by reason of history, geological formations, or ecological resources. *See also* park; preserve.

National Park Service   Federal agency responsible for the proper management and operation of the system of national parks in the United States.

National Passenger Traffic Association (NPTA)   Professional association of corporate travel managers.

National Recreation and Parks Association (NRPA)   Professional association of recreation facility leaders, park managers, and educators concerned with the development, patterns of use, and proper management of public and private recreation and park facilities.

National Restaurant Association (NRA)   Professional trade association dedicated to the special concerns of the foodservice operator via educational programs and governmental lobbying.

National Tour Brokers Association (NTBA)   Membership association of motorcoach tour operators licensed by the Interstate Commerce Commission.

national tourism organization   Office entrusted with the responsibility to formulate and implement the tourism policy for a nation. May be a ministry, department, commission, directorate general, or board.

national tourism policy   Proposal, at present pending in Congress, to establish a national tourism policy council to coordinate federal programs and policies affecting the tourism industry, and to develop a marketing plan to stimulate travel to the United States by residents of other countries.

National Transportation Safety Board (NTSB)   Agency of the Department of Transportation responsible for developing safety standards for public transportation, and investigating all accidents involving such transportation.

NATO *See* National Association of Travel Organizations.

natural areas Places of natural beauty created by vegetation or geological formation, and not commercially developed.

nautical mile Used to measure sea and air navigation distance; equal to one minute of latitude, approximately 6,076 feet.

navigable airspace Airspace above the minimum altitude of flight prescribed by regulations issued by the FAA, including airspace needed to ensure safety in takeoff and landing.

need-satisfaction selling Strategy of selling that involves the use of probing questions, recognition of nonverbal messages, verbal support, and other interview techniques so as to increase the percentages of both sales and satisfied customers. The travel agent as well as the intangible products of tourism are regarded as ideal opportunities for this type of sales approach.

Neptune Roman god of the sea. *See also* crossing the line.

net fares Competitive pricing strategy for scheduled airlines, which came about as part of the CAB deregulation process. *Bulk fares,* more correctly contract bulk fares, are one type of net fare pricing allowing for the retail sale of scheduled airline services at prices other than those of an airline's tariff. The CAB requested experimentation so as to gather information on the effect of deregulation; in response, some airlines have offered discounts for cash, added a surcharge for credit card use, and other variations of pricing.

net rate Wholesale rate that is marked up for resale to the customer.

net tourist income *See* income, net tourism.

new colonialism Usually a negative term describing a tendency of tourism to take over a region for its special purpose, displacing the region's original residents.

NIFI *See* National Institute for the Foodservice Industry.

night audit Updating of all current guest account records, including verification of all entries. Derived from the practice of the auditor completing this work at night when the property is relatively quiet.

night club Facility that offers professional stage show entertainment as its main attraction. The customers pay for this service by means of a cover charge or as a function of their bar, liquor, or food charge.

no-frill Condition or class of service that offers no extra items or conveniences. Basic service, with no extras included in the price.

no go Usually refers to a flight that fails to depart as scheduled, but can also be applied to a train, bus, or other scheduled transportation.

no-host *See* cash bar.

non-sked *See* supplemental airline.

nonstop   Transportation service between two destination points with no scheduled stops between the points.

no rate specified   Usually refers to a steamship or cruise booking in which the line has guaranteed the reservation, but at the time of confirmation is unable to assign a cabin or specify a rate.

no-show   Guest, client, or passenger who fails to use or to cancel a reservation.

nouvelle cuisine   Gourmet style of food preparation which strives to replicate the taste and attention to detail of classic French cuisine while also reducing calories using contemporary ingredients and modern preparation equipment.

NPTA   *See* National Passenger Traffic Association.

NRA   *See* National Restaurant Association.

NRPA   *See* National Recreation and Parks Association.

NRS   *See* no rate specified.

NTBA   *See* National Tour Brokers Association.

NTSB   *See* National Transportation Safety Board.

NV   Nuclear Vessel.

O

observation car   Railroad car specially designed for sightseeing; also called *dome car* or *bubble car.*

observation point   Area or structure provided to afford the user an unobstructed or special view of some scene or activity.

occupancy rate   Percentage derived by dividing the total number of rooms occupied during a given time period (night, week, year) by the total number of rooms available for occupancy during that time period.

offering   Advertised product, service, tour, or package for sale.

off-line   Any carrier facility or function located or performed other than on the carrier's certified route.

off-peak rate   Discounted hotel rate or fare applied at a time that is not busy.

off-season   Season or seasons of the year when an area's tourism business is slow or minimal.

OJ   *See* open jaw.

one way trip   Term generally used to identify a commercial transportation ticket purchase that does not include, at the time of purchase, arrangements for returning to the point of origin. *See also* trip.

on-off sales   Identifies a liquor establishment licensed to sell and serve by the glass for consumption on the premises, and to sell by the package for consumption elsewhere.

open bar   Liquor service for a party or group that does not require individual payment for each drink. The total cost is absorbed in some other way, usually by the sponsoring individual or group.

open commissions   *See* open pay.

open jaw   Round trip or round trip itinerary or ticket in which the departure point is different from the arrival point; a trip from Chicago to New York with a return from Boston to Chicago would be an open jaw.

open pay   Part of the CAB deregulation process, whereby the travel agent's pay or commission rates paid by the domestic airlines will be "open" to variety as negotiated by the parties concerned (or as offered by the supplier) rather than specified by the CAB. Also known as *open commission.*

open rate   Applicable to specified routes for which traffic conferences have failed to agree on a uniform rate. In such situations the carriers are free to establish their own rates.

open space   Land allowed to remain in a natural condition, or an area affording a panoramic view. In buildings, areas designed to give a feeling of spaciousness.

open ticket   Ticket that does not specify the date on which a certain service is to be performed, leaving the passenger to secure a reservation at a later date.

operating company   Organization that manages one or more hotels, restaurants, or similar properties.

operation   Place of business.

operator   Owner or manager of a place of business.

optional   Choice of taking or not taking the service mentioned. Usually there is an additional charge, which is not included in the basic price.

origin   Point where the passenger begins an itinerary.

outdoor museum   *See* living history attraction.

outfitter   Commercial business that provides a person with the equipment necessary for an activity or experience.

overbooking   Deliberate or mistaken confirmation of more reservations than there are seats or rooms. *See* oversale.

overcrowding   Condition of having too many people using a specific area or facility.

override   Extra commission paid by carriers, wholesale tour operators, hotels, and so forth to travel agents as bonuses or incentives.

oversale   Sale of more seats, or acceptance of more reservations for rooms, than space actually available. Sometimes used to compensate for the expected percentage of no-shows.

oversupply Consequence of overproduction or of diminished demand; too much of a product or service for the existing demand.

P

Pacific Area Travel Association (PATA) Membership organization of government and private business representatives that seeks to promote and monitor travel to and within the Pacific area.

package Prearranged combination of elements. In most cases a package consists of many of the same activities and services the customer would normally purchase, but the package price results in a savings for the customer. Packages are developed as a service for customers, a means of promoting business in slow business periods, and as a way of introducing new services and products. Examples include room-food weekend packages, fly-drive packages theater-restaurant packages, etc. *See also* tour.

packager *See* wholesale tour operator.

package tour *See* tour.

page To call for someone, especially a guest, by means of a loudspeaker or other electronic device. In past years, the practice of having an employee walk through the property calling out the name of the guest.

parador Castles, abbeys, or other scenic or historic buildings that have been rehabilitated for use as hotels.

paratransit system People-moving system that can be adjusted to changing travel patterns and travel demands; includes jitneys, taxis, car pools, and buses.

park Area set aside for public use, to be maintained by public funds. Parks are usually created as a way to preserve some unique natural habitat for enjoyment by future generations as well as to facilitate the nondestructive recreational use of the area. The significance of the unique area as well as the source of funds differentiates a national park from a state or city park. *Pocket parks* are small recreational areas of green space (trees, grass, flowerbeds, and so forth) located within an urban area. *Underwater parks* involve the preservation of underwater reefs, lagoons, and adjacent shorelines. *See also* national park; preserve; theme park.

parlor Hotel room not used as a bedroom but rather as a sitting room; sometimes referred to as a *salon*.

parlor car Railroad car with individual swivel seats and food and bar service. *See also* railroad classes of service (U.S.A. and Canada).

participant One who takes active part in an activity.

party Customer or group of customers to be serviced in the same way; members of the same tour group.

passenger   Person being transported or scheduled to be transported by any carrier or vehicle, excluding the driver; usually limited to a person who has paid a required fee for or purchased a ticket.

passenger mile   One passenger carried one mile; computed by multiplying the number of vehicle miles traveled by the number of passengers transported.

passenger service agent   Usually an airline employee, assisting passengers with check-in and boarding procedures at the airport.

passenger service representative   Usually an airline employee, assisting passengers at the airport by providing information, directions, assisting the elderly, arranging ground transportation, and so forth.

passenger, through   Passenger scheduled to continue a journey on the same vehicle—though it makes intermediate stops.

passenger traffic manager (PTM)   Employee responsible for making travel arrangements for other employees of the same company.

passenger, transfer   Person scheduled to change aircraft or vehicles on the way to some destination.

passenger, transit   Person traveling via an itinerary which includes one or more stops in foreign countries which are not the person's destination. At each stop the person may leave the plane or even change planes or wait for the next scheduled flight without officially entering the country by going through customs procedures.

passport   Official government documentation of the identity and citizenship of an individual. Required for travel abroad and for return.

PATA   *See* Pacific Area Travel Association.

PATCO   *See* Professional Air Traffic Controllers Organization.

patron   Customer or client, particularly on a regular basis, of a business establishment.

payload   In commercial transportation, the portion of the total weight or total load that produces revenue, be it passengers, cargo, or a combination of both.

peak density   Number of persons accommodated at a resort area, etc. during a busy period; an indicator of facility capacity.

peak fare   *See* peak use period.

peak rate   *See* peak use period.

peak season   *See* high season; peak use period.

peak use period   Time of the day, week, or season of the year when facilities are used intensively, perhaps to a point of overloading them. Holidays, especially Christmas, are peak-use periods for many airports; hot summer weekends result in peak use for beaches. Peak-use periods often involve peak or premium rates; that is, special rates or fares.

peaks and valleys   *See* seasonality.

pension *See* boarding house; full pension; half pension.

people movers Wide range of motorized vehicles and platforms capable of moving great numbers of people small distances in a short time, be it to and from a terminal and a waiting aircraft, moving sidewalks, or a shuttle bus.

people pollution Deterioration of a tourist destination, caused by large numbers of visitors that overcrowd existing facilities.

per diem Amount of money paid by a company to an employee who travels; intended to cover daily expenses.

perquisites Compensation or benefits from an employer or because of an employment position above and beyond one's salary. Commonly referred to as "perks."

person-night Occupancy/income statistic; one paying guest staying one night. A group of three people staying in the same room one night would equal three person-nights.

petit dèjeuner Continental breakfast.

pickup camper Pick-up truck which has been fitted with a structure that fits over the bed of the truck, creating an enclosure suitable for sleeping and storage of camping items.

pictograms Means of communicating the presence of needed services by use of symbol-pictures (pictograms), which tend to overcome language barriers. Road signs that use no English or any other language are pictograms.

pilgrimage Travel to and for the purpose of visiting a location regarded as sacred by the traveler.

pilot 1. Person who flies an aircraft; 2. Person with expert local knowledge who takes charge of a ship entering or leaving the port or area.

pitch 1. See-saw up and down motion of a ship or aircraft; 2. Distance between the front of one aircraft seat and the front of the seat behind it.

planning Rational system of procedures proposed for achieving a desired goal. A plan must involve a. objectives, understood and accepted by those involved, b. a program, leading to the objectives, and c. the measurement of progress toward the objectives.

play Free, spontaneous activity; synonymous with recreation. An activity done for its own sake, rather than for economic gain. Tourism may be considered a form of play.

play environment Area or facility exclusively designed for fun and enjoyment. Theme parks, sports stadiums, resorts, and tourist destination areas are examples of play environments.

pleasure places Commercial and noncommercial recreation facilities in an area, including public parks, restaurants, theaters, and the like.

point of call For an air transport, an intermediate stop in the itinerary at which the flight lands for traffic purposes. *See* port of call.

point of origin City, country or airport where a person begins an itinerary.

point-of-purchase (POP) POPs are displays or advertising intended to encourage immediate on-premise sales.

point-to-point Term for basic transportation only. A point-to-point sale covers only the cost of the ticket; a point-to-point fare is the basic rate from one city to another.

policy Identification of overall or specific goals and strategies as stated by a governmental body. Policy statements help to orient those involved in the planning process.

political action committee Method of political involvement. A PAC collects voluntary contributions from its members and donates the collected funds to political candidates and causes it supports. A number of tourism and hospitality companies have formed such groups.

port Left side of a ship or aircraft, looking forward; originally called larboard. *See also* starboard; port of call; port of entry.

porter Employee of a railroad terminal or airline terminal, who carries passengers' baggage in return for a gratuity. Also called a *skycap* or *redcap*.

porterage Baggage handling; a guest or passenger service that may or may not be included in the price of the tour.

portion control Methods used by commercial food service establishments to provide even-sized portions to all customers so as to treat all fairly and keep control over food costs.

port of call Scheduled port at which a vessel calls regularly.

port of entry Officially designated port where foreign passengers or goods may enter a country.

posh Originally meant "port out—starboard home" indicating the most favorable location for a steamship cabin from Britain to the Far East. The passenger would occupy accommodations on the shady (north) and therefore cooler side of the ship. *Posh* now means snobbish, high class, exclusive.

positioning Moving an aircraft, ship, bus, or other transport vehicle, to a location where it will again begin revenue service.

prefabricated construction Construction technique that uses production line techniques. Structures are partly constructed under optimum conditions and then moved and completed on the final site thus saving time and money. Tourism facilities increasingly use this method.

prejudice Biased attitude or opinion of a person or group, created or influenced by one's culture and experiences. Because tourism is an industry based on images, expectations, and contrasts it is sometimes the setting for prejudice, often in the form of favorable or unfavorable simplified statements about tourists from a given country or city, residents of an area, a category of employees, and the like.

prepaid extra nights Additional nights included in a hotel voucher over and above the number of nights included in the basic package tour. Rates for extra nights are normally published next to the rate for the package tour itself.

prepaid ticket advice (PTA) Form used by air carriers to indicate that payment for air transportation has been made in a different place than that where the transportation commences.

pre/post convention tour Extension of a convention tour whereby for an additional charge, extra days or destinations may be added to the beginning or end of a basic convention itinerary.

preregistration Service provided especially for conventions, tours and large meetings, where a significant portion of the registration process, such as room assignment, filling out of guest registration cards, is completed before the guest's arrival. The term also applies to a situation where the guest, customer or meeting participant is requested to register before arrival (preregister) so as to decrease the amount of paper work necessary upon arrival. Such a request often includes the added incentive of a preregistration price, which is less than that which will be due from those registering at the door.

preserve Area of trees or grassland designated by a government to remain in its natural condition; usually located in and around urban areas as a buffer and a recreation resource. *See also* national park; park.

primitive Popularly used in tourism to describe a culture, destination, or facility that is supposedly less complex than what the visitor is normally accustomed to.

principal Primary producer or supplier of a tourism good or service; the person or company assuming primary responsibility for all or some part of a travel program.

prix fixe Price of a table d'hote meal; a fixed price for a complete meal as described, with no substitutions permitted.

productivity Measurement of the ratio of input to output; a measurement of efficiency.

Professional Air Traffic Controllers Organization (PATCO) Union of FAA traffic control employees.

professional liability insurance Financial protection for travel agents and other suppliers against lawsuits from tourists and other involved parties.

profit center Revenue-generating activities of a property, such as a bar, restaurant, or room sales. The success of such activities may depend upon the existence of numerous amenities and services that do not directly generate a profit, such as a spacious lobby or free airport transfers.

promotion Efforts of a company or destination area to create and maintain a favorable public image. Also called *promo*. *See also* promotional mix.

promotional fare *See* fare.

promotional mix Any combination of advertising, personal selling, sales promotion, and public relations intended to sell a product or service.

proof of citizenship Document establishing the nationality of a traveler.

promenade deck On a passenger ship, an upper deck enclosed by glass.

protected commissions A supplier or tour wholesaler guarantee to pay commissions to travel agents, and provide full refunds to all clients holding prepaid confirmed reservations, even if the cruise, tour, or other commissionable activity is cancelled.

protective tariff Tax designed to protect a country's producers; it is levied on competing imports.

provisioned charter Rental of a boat or yacht where the price includes all fuel and provisions but no crew. *See also* bareboat charter.

psychic cost/psychic income *Psychic cost* is the emotional price paid for engaging in an activity, as the boredom of a necessary job; *psychic income* is the enjoyment gained from an activity, whether work or leisure.

PTA *See* prepaid ticket advice.

PTM *See* passenger traffic manager.

public charter (PC) Charter fare created by the CAB which replaced the one-stop charter (OTC), the three-stop inclusive tour charter (ITC), and the air-only advance booking charter (ABC).

Pullman Railroad sleeping and parlor car used in North America. *See also* railroad classes of service (Europe); railroad classes of service (U.S.A. and Canada).

purser Person responsible for all hotel and financial functions of a passenger ship, and for the service and care of the passengers.

purveyor One who provides or supplies a product or service, whether at the wholesale or retail level.

push/pull theory Tourism theory which identifies the "push" exerted on the tourist by factors such as employment, community, and personal life—a force that impels him to seek change, challenge, recreation. This combines with the "pull" of attractive locations and activities.

Q

QSS Quadruple Screw Steamship.

quad Room suitable for occupancy by four persons.

quality Substance, meaning, or extent of lasting effects of a given experience; an imprecise, emotional, and often strictly personal estimation of the perceived value of an event. A concept used in discussions of tourism: quality of the tourism experience, quality of the tourism product, quality of life.

R

R and R   Rest and recreation, also known as rest and relaxation. Originally described a military leave program; more recently used to describe short-stay vacation packages. Also, the periods of free time built into planned tours.

rack rate   Regular published rates of a hotel or other tourism service.

railroad classes of service (Europe)   *Third Class*—Least expensive unreserved seating.   *Second Class*—Unreserved seating, sometimes reserved at extra charge. *First Class*—Larger seats, sometimes reserved at extra charge. *Pullman*—Reserved seating car on British trains. *Couchette*—Various class compartment configurations of 4 to 6 people each with a seat/berth, a sheet, blanket and pillow but no toilet or sink. *Sleeping Car*—First and second class service with berths for 2 or 3 people, toilet, and sink.

railroad classes of service (U.S.A. and Canada)   *Coach*—Unreserved seating. *Reserved Coach*—Assigned seating. *Parlor Car*—Individual swivel seats, food and liquor service. *Upper Berth*—Top bed in slumber coach, Pullman or sleeping car. *Lower Berth*—Bottom bed in slumber coach, Pullman, or sleeping car. *Roomette*—Small bedroom with toilet and sink. *Bedroom*—Bedroom for 2 people with separate toilet and sink. *Bedroom Suite*—Two adjoining bedrooms for up to 4 people. Also called a double bedroom. *Drawing Room*—Larger bedroom for up to three people. *Compartment*—Lower berth on Pullman with upper berth folded up or a separate room seating up to 6 people with separate toilet and sink.

Rail Travel Promotion Association (RTPA)   Now superseded by AMTRAK, the RTPA coordinated and promoted railroad package tours.

ramp   Staircase on wheels used to load and unload an aircraft. *See also* gangway; jetway.

ramp agent   Airline employee who loads and unloads baggage, cargo, and food supplies on to an aircraft.

rate   Price or cost of a given service. Usually implies necessity of approval of prices by some regulatory agency.

rate hike   Announced increase in fares or other charges for product or services. Usually implies necessity of approval of changes by a regulatory agency, and that such increases will be widely published.

ready foods   Specific type of convenience food, which has been processed and prepared to the point where it can be kept in storage until immediately prior to service. Ready foods need only to be heated and served, as in the case of hamburgers, stew, and chicken.

rebate   Practice of charging less than the posted tariff, with the result that someone makes or saves money as an inducement to sell or purchase. It is illegal for airlines to rebate, that is, charge the travel agent less than the tariff filed with the CAB. Similarly, it is at least questionable for a hotel to lower the price of its rooms in a way that is secret and often denied if discovered.

receiving agent   *See* contractor.

receiving airline   Air carrier that will transport a passenger after his arrival at some point in his itinerary.

receiving country   One that has more foreign visitors from another country than citizens that travel to that country. Also, a country that receives more visitors than it generates.

reception agency   *See* contractor.

recipe   Detailed formula specifying ingredients, proportions, combination sequence, and preparation method to result in a food. A *standardized recipe* is the result of a detailed analysis of the entire process by which raw ingredients are transformed into a finished plated-for-service product. It is recorded on cards or other devices in such detail that a relatively untrained person can consistently prepare an acceptable product.

reconfirmation   Action attesting to one's intention to utilize a reservation. An international airline passenger is required to reconfirm a reserved seat on subsequent flights if a stopover exceeds a certain time limit or the seat may be legally resold. Hotels and most other tourism services suggest reconfirmation, especially when the initial reservation was made well in advance.

recreation   Diverse activities freely chosen, excluding those activities connected with work. *Commercial recreation* is the provision of means for a pleasurable activity for the purpose of making a profit. *Public recreation* is the provision of similar means, financed and usually managed by a government agency.

recreational development   Any complex of facilities and services oriented toward recreational use.

recreational facilities   The numerous specific services, both commercial and public, which are needed in a recreational area.

recreation center   Place or structure where equipment and facilities for leisure activities may be obtained, and where such activities may be pursued.

recreation vehicle (RV)   1. Any motorized self-contained camping trailer or mobile home used by its owners as a combined means of transport/accommodations while traveling; 2. A truck or van, especially equipped for off-road pleasure driving and use; 3. Cars and motorcycles modified for the express purpose of permitting the rider to have an unusual and pleasurable experience (example: dune buggies, off-road motorbikes).

red light district   Area of a city known for entertainment of questionable taste, including the availability of houses of prostitution.

refreshment bar   Commercial food service facility located in transport terminals and other high volume, fast-paced facilities, offering the customer a limited variety of alcoholic or nonalcoholic beverages and snacks to be consumed while standing at a counter.

regatta   Water carnival.

regionalism Tendency of groups of people organized into communities, neighborhoods, or some other social entity to share values, norms, expectations and in general, a way of life which may differ significantly from other such groupings, within the same geographic, legal or national boundaries. The concept is especially useful for the person who enters the area as a would-be businessperson, developer, or tourist entertaining an oversimplified image that all of the people and communities in a nation think in the same way.

regional planning Systematic approach to designing for and influencing the direction of the future of a specific geographical area. The area is regarded as a *region,* that is, a significant and identifiable physical and social unit with an interrelated way of life which is to be encouraged and enhanced.

registration 1. Process of signing in at the front desk of a hotel, or motel, often involving some check of the guest's ability to pay for the room; 2. Process by which qualified individuals are listed on an official roster maintained by a governmental or nongovernmental agency. Historically, used interchangeably with the term *certification.* Certification is more appropriately used when attesting to a certain level of professional competency. Registration is more appropriately used to describe the process by which the certified or licensed individuals are listed on an official roster.

registry Country in which a ship is registered. This may not be, and often is not, the country of ownership. For example, a ship may be British-owned but registered in a foreign country, such as Panama, Liberia, or the Bahamas. The certificate of registration does not attest to a vessel's quality, safety, or to the nationality or skill of its crew.

regular Patron, guest, or customer who is recognized as being a repeat customer.

regulatory agency Government, international, or trade agency with authority to regulate the actions of the businesses falling under jurisdiction of the agency.

relative deprivation Discrepancy between what a person expects and what is actually attained. Describes the relationships of two dynamics; a person can feel deprived or "worse off" even with an objective increase in real wages or real buying power because his aspirations and expectations have increased at an even faster rate.

rep Representative (rep). Individual or company authorized to act as a representative for a supplier or other business.

repeat customer/tourist/visitor Special category of customer who is at least partly motivated by the experience of one or more previous visits to the business or area. The long-term success of any business is based upon the ability to create repeat customers.

reservation Written or oral communication to hold a room, seat, or place for a customer, as requested by the customer. A promise of service. Also known as a *booking.* A *duplicate reservation* refers to two or more reservations held by the same customer for substantially the same flight destination, hotel, or other reserved space event. *See also* guaranteed reservation.

reservationist Employee of a tourism company, such as an airline or a tour operator, who accepts and confirms reservations.

reserved coach *See* railroad classes of service (U.S.A. and Canada).

reserved seat Seat or space that has or can be specifically assigned to an individual for a given period of time, be it a single performance, a flight, a ride, a meal, or a season.

residential hotel Commercial accommodation specializing in providing the services appropriate for the customer who plans to stay for a month, a season, or longer.

resort Geographic or business area offering a variety of facilities, services, and activities for the accommodation, use, and enjoyment of visitors.

resort community *See* resort town.

resort hotel *See* hotel.

resort tax *See* room tax.

resort town Community that is part of, or so close as to be appreciably influenced by, a major tourist destination area. In seasonal tourism localities the town may significantly change in services, population size, and character in direct relation to the tourist flow.

responsibility clause Detailed statement of conditions applicable to the sale of a tour package; one of the printed sections on a tour brochure.

rest area Area, often provided as a public service, located immediately adjacent to a major feeder roadway, where travelers may stop, use restroom facilities, and in some cases get information on road conditions and nearby attractions.

restaurant Room, building, or place where meals are served or sold to customers.

restaurant industry Descriptive phrase for all types of commercial food service, including restaurants as well as contract feeding and institutional feeding operations.

restaurateur Owner or manager of a restaurant.

rest stop Practice of periodically stopping for a break or rest while traveling by automobile, or by motorcoach, often in conjunction with a need to get fuel, food, or use restroom facilities. *See* rest area.

retail agency *See* travel agency.

retailer Retail travel agent. An agent who sells products and services to the public.

retirement migration Tendency of some people to move from the area they lived in most of their employed life to the area they often visited when on vacation.

retrofit Technological modification of an already produced item, be it an aircraft engine or a restaurant oven, so as to incorporate desired or required changes.

return   Round trip.

return on investment   Statistic found by dividing a business' net income by the total amount of money invested in the business. Applied to tourism, it is important to note that every business, government, community, and customer consciously or unconsciously uses some version of this concept in evaluating the consequences of any expenditure.

revalidation sticker   Official notice that a change of the original reservation has been made; affixed to the flight coupon of an air ticket.

revenue   Income earned by a company by selling its product or service.

revenue passenger mile   One paying passenger carried one mile in commercial transport service.

riviera   Originally a famous resort region along the coast of the Mediterranean from Marseilles in southern France to La Spezia in northern Italy. More generally used to identify a number of sea coast resort areas thought to offer a luxurious and exclusive lifestyle and facilities.

RMS   Royal Mail Steamship.

road map   Printed guide for the automobile-using tourist indicating the communities, roads, and distances involved.

roadside emergency telephone   Readily identifiable telephones located along roadways for use by travelers.

roomette   *See* railroad classes of service (U.S.A. and Canada).

rooming house   Similar to a boarding house except that no food is provided. Rooms are usually shared, rented for longer than one night, and very low cost.

room occupancy rate   *See* occupancy rate.

room rate   Price or cost of renting a given room in a commercial accommodation. The rate is often published and variable depending upon the number of people and the season of the year.

room service   Food and beverage delivery to the guest's room.

room tax   Municipal or region-imposed tax levied upon the user of a hotel or motel room. Varied in form, it may be a percentage, a flat-use fee, or a per day fee. In some cases it is a source of revenue for area promotion groups or area beautification projects.

rope tow   Motorized heavy moving rope that skiers hold in their hands, providing transport. *See* cable transporters.

routing service   Free or for fee service provided by many oil companies, credit card companies, and automobile clubs, whereby alternative highway routes to a specific destination are identified for the person requesting the service. Road conditions, mileage between points, and sightseeing suggestions, as well as maps and brochures, are provided.

RTPA   *See* Rail Travel Promotion Association.

run-of-the-house-rate   Flat rate for which a hotel or motel agrees to offer any of its available rooms to a group.

rush periods   Times in the operation of a business or an area where there are relatively greater numbers of customers than at other times. For a restaurant the rush may be the lunch and dinner hours; for a ski resort it might be Christmas week, or the weekends in comparison to weekdays.

Russian service   Style of formal dinner service where the waiter removes the dishes used for one course before the next course arrives.

RV   *See* recreation vehicle.

S

sailing permit   Income tax clearance certificate issued by the Internal Revenue Service. Required for all resident aliens before departure from the United States to a foreign country.

sales aid   Brochures, giveaway maps, inexpensive novelties, and other materials that help to make a sale.

sales office   Facility or office for the sale of a service or tickets to be exchanged for a service. Sales offices are usually located in an area convenient to the customer but at a distance from where the service is to be rendered. For example, an airline ticket office would be located in a city center, or a Las Vegas hotel sales office might be located in major cities such as Chicago or New York.

sales promotion   Activity, other than advertising and personal selling, aimed at stimulating the sale of goods and services. Included are contests, trade show exhibits, agent seminars, and so forth.

salon   *See* parlor.

sample room   Hotel or motel room which is rented by a customer for the purpose of displaying a company's merchandise rather than for sleeping.

SATH   *See* Society for Advancement of Travel for the Handicapped.

SATO   *See* South American Tourism Organization.

SATW   *See* Society of American Travel Writers.

scenic lookout   *See* observation point.

scenic route   Path, road, or highway which exists as an alternative to some other more time-efficient route to the same desired destination but which offers the user a relatively more visually enjoyable experience.

schedule   Booklet or chart showing scheduled departure and arrival times, dates and days of service, classes of service, and fares for airlines, railroads, bus companies, steamship and cruise lines, and so forth.

scheduled airline   Any airline providing scheduled service for passengers or cargo.

scheduled airline ticket office   Office operated and staffed by scheduled airlines for booking official government business and the private travel of government employees.

scheduled service   Any form of transport service operated over a carrier's certificated routes in accordance with published schedules.

sea legs   Ability to walk on the deck of a ship while it is pitching or rolling. More generally, ability to tolerate the movement of a ship or other vessel. Also, resistance to seasickness.

seaside resort   Commercial multiactivity/service tourism facility located on the shores of a sea or ocean. *See* resort.

seasonality   Patterned fluctuations in market demand due to the time-of-year specifics of the area's attractions, e.g., snow skiing, water sports, spring festivals, and/or competing patterned demands on the customer, e.g., school year, traditional scheduling of paid vacations in the summer.

seasonal rates   Pricing structure allowing for variation of prices for the same service depending upon the time of the year.

seat pitch   Distance between the front of one aircraft seat and the front of the seat behind it.

second class   *See* railroad classes of service (Europe).

second class hotel   Economy or tourist class accommodations offering few services and amenities.

second home   Privately owned house that is used by the owners as a place for recreation and enjoyment on weekends and whenever they can get away. Also referred to as a *vacation home* or *summer home*.

segment   One part of a trip; travel between any two points on a multidestination itinerary; also called a *leg*.

self drive   Automobile rented without a driver. Also called *U-drive*.

self-service   Form of service where the guest must help himself to some extent. Favored by some guests as a freedom from service, this form of operation reduces employee numbers and costs and, therefore, the prices paid by the customer.

seller's market   Supply-demand condition where the demand for a product or service exceeds the existing supply. Prices may rise as a consequence. The peak season or high season of a resort area is an example.

selling up   Strategy of increasing the customer's final bill by successfully suggesting items or services that the customer may have overlooked. Examples include dessert, car rental, travel insurance.

Senate Tourism Caucus   Bipartisan body of U.S. Senators who serve to monitor the progress of legislation having an influence on tourism. *See also* House Congressional Tourism Caucus.

senior citizen   Description of a market segment generally involving persons over sixty years of age.

service charge   1. Amount of money, determined by a percentage of a customer's total purchase, which is automatically added to the bill. The service charge replaces the "voluntary" gratuity or tip; 2. A rare additional charge made by travel agents for services beyond the normal activities of arranging for transport, accommodations, and so forth.

set menu   *See* menu.

setup   1. The providing at a guest's table at a price, the ice, glasses, and nonalcoholic mixers to go with the liquor the guest has brought into the restaurant from home or purchased elsewhere; often a legal strategy in areas that forbid the sale of liquor in restaurants; 2. The providing of sufficient quantities of ice, glasses, mixers, and liquor to each table, for the guests to serve themselves. This form of setup is common at parties, where the host is charged for the total of liquor consumed.

shell   *See* tour shell.

shift   Group of people who work together during the same time period; also, the time period itself as in night shift, or morning shift.

ship   Seagoing vessel of substantial size navigating deep water. Also used to refer to an aircraft. *See also* boat; dinghy; liner; yacht.

shore excursion   Planned tour available for purchase by passengers at scheduled stops of a cruise itinerary.

shoulder period   Calendar period between a peak season and an off-season, usually favored by a promotional fare or rate which is lower than peak and higher than off-season.

shuttle service   Provision of transportation from one point to another for both people and baggage. Usually over short distances, as from aircraft to terminal, and basic in nature.

sico bed   Bed that folds into the wall out of sight when not in use, providing more room space.

side trip   1. Arranged tour package offered as an option to participants of a tour; 2. Independent diversion from a major tour or itinerary to a point of interest not included in the tour.

single   Reservation for one person; a room or other facility for use by one person.

single service   Use of disposable items used once and then discarded to avoid the costs of handling, cleaning, and so forth. Paper placemats and napkins are examples.

single supplement   Additional amount of money to be paid by a client for single occupancy of a hotel room, especially when participating in a tour that specifies double occupancy accommodations.

SITE   *See* Society of Incentive Travel Executives.

site   Specific location; specific area.

sitting   On some cruise ships the dining room is too small to accommodate all passengers at the same time; passengers have to be served in two groups, *early sitting* and *late sitting.*

sitting room ensuite   Sitting room connecting to a bedroom.

SKAL Club   Social organization of travel industry executives. Derived from the Danish and Norwegian word *skoal*—"to your health."

skeleton itinerary   *See* stripped package.

skilled labor   Persons with specialized skills or training for a specific occupation.

skip   Guest of a hotel, restaurant, or other commercial facility who leaves without checking out or paying the bill.

skycap   Porter or luggage carrier at an airport terminal.

skyjacking   *See* aircraft piracy.

sleeper seat   Transport seating designed to recline to an almost horizontal position, thus approximating a bed. Available as a luxury-cost option on some forms of long-distance transportation.

slip   Individual docking space in a marina where a yacht or boat is moored.

smuggle   Importing or exporting goods secretly without payment of required duty.

sneeze guard   Protective glass or plastic barrier placed at face level around food displays such as buffet tables.

sociability   Human interaction engaged in for pleasure rather than profit or practical consequence. The interaction is its own justification.

social   Interaction of individual and group in human community. *Social change* refers to variations or modifications in the social process; it may be planned or not, temporary or permanent, beneficial or harmful. *Social disintegration* is the loss of common interests and consequent breakup of a social group or community. *Social disorganization* describes a loss of agreed-on goals and standards, and resulting uncoordinated behavior. *Social indicators* are data sources used to measure community wellbeing; they may include such things as statistics on marriages and divorces, or on juvenile delinquency. *Social planning* describes the use of relevant psychological and sociological factors in organizing policy and implementation of community goals. *Social progress* is change in the direction of a recognized and approved goal.

social distance   Conceptual indicator of the similarity/difference in social position and experiences of persons or groups. Concept is valuable in tourism as a means of anticipating the probability of successes or problems in a situation where tourists from different backgrounds will be together as on a tour or where area residents and tourists will be required to interact.

social dualism   A problematic societal condition where behavior similar to that of an industrialized society exists side by side with traditional behavior. Applied to tourism, the almost complete lack of contact between two or more social groups is most evident in areas where traditional agriculture coexists with modern resort areas.

Society for Advancement of Travel for the Handicapped (SATH) Nonprofit organization attempting to increase the opportunities for travel for the handicapped by proposing legislation and technical changes that would reduce the existing barriers to such travel, and by informing the handicapped person of available travel services and experiences.

Society of American Travel Writers (SATW) Professional association of persons who write travel books and travel articles.

Society of Incentive Travel Executives (SITE) Membership trade association of agents who specialize in incentive travel packages.

soiree Party held in the evening.

sommelier Wine steward; wine waiter.

South American Tourism Organization (SATO) Association of government and private companies seeking to promote and monitor travel to and within the nations of South America.

souvenir Object—be it a purchased artifact, found object or photograph —that serves to help a person recall a travel experience. Utility is not a prime consideration.

spa *See* health resort.

space Reserved or reservable room, seat, table, and so forth.

space available Literally, if the space is available. Often a reduced fare or charge category in which the service will be provided if space is available.

special interest group *See* special interest tour.

special interest tour Prearranged, packaged, itinerary designed to appeal to or respond to a request by a group of persons with unique interests. Such a tour may focus on horticulture, law, gourmet dining, backpacking, music, religious events, sports, or any other specific field.

Special Travel Industry Council on Energy Conservation (STICEC) Industry and government representatives charged with exploring alternative methods of energy conservation and estimating the impact such methods would have on the tourism industry.

specialty vehicle Unusual forms of transportation offered for rent, hire, or use by tourists. Includes courtesy vans, jeeps, rickshaws, two-seat bikes, paddle boats.

specification Detailed, accurate description of product to be supplied. Used to ensure consistent quality.

spectator One who observes others' activity, rather than participating in such activity.

speed trap Questionable practice of hiding or locating law enforcement officers in pursuit vehicles at a roadway point where automobile drivers are legally required but unlikely to rapidly reduce their traveling speed.

split shift   Employee scheduling in which the employee is scheduled to work only during the busy or rush periods of the day (as lunch or dinner in a restaurant) with required time off from work between the two periods.

SS   Steamship

SST   *See* aircraft.

standard of living   Necessities, comforts, and luxuries that a given society views as essential for wellbeing. A comparative concept by which one's way of life is related to that of other people. Employment generated by tourism may be intended to raise an area's standard of living while also introducing new comforts and luxuries, which may raise expectations. Pleasure travel is regarded as a consequence of a relatively high standard of living.

standard ticket stock   *See* ticket stock.

standby   Customer waiting for space (a seat, a room) to become available.

starboard   Right side of a ship or aircraft, looking forward. The name is derived from the time when ships were steered by a steering board, which was located at the right side of the ship. *See also* port.

star rating system   *See* hotel classifications.

stateroom   Accommodations on board a passenger or cruise ship.

state travel office   Governmental office of state or territory generally responsible for coordinating and publicizing tourism opportunities within the state for state residents and nonresidents.

statute mile   5,280 feet. *See also* air mile; nautical mile.

steward   On board ship the *chief steward* is in charge of all catering and household services and personnel; the *dining room steward* is usually the table waiter; the *room steward* is the passenger's housekeeper in the cabin; the *deck steward* is in charge of deck services such as deck chairs, blankets, and dispensing morning bouillon and afternoon tea. On board an aircraft, the *cabin steward* is responsible for the care and feeding of the passengers.

STICEC   *See* Special Travel Industry Council on Energy Conservation.

stiffing   Deliberate withholding of a tip or gratuity when it is expected and deserved.

stopover   Scheduled or intentional interruption of a journey.

strand   Abandoning of passengers or tour clients at the beginning or any time during a prepaid travel program.

stretch jet   *See* aircraft.

stripped package   Minimum tour package designed primarily to qualify for an IT number, permitting the seller to receive a higher commission. Also known as a *skeleton itinerary*. *See also* IT number.

structural unemployment   Unemployment resulting when certain skills are no longer required because of major changes in a nation's or region's economy. Also used to describe unemployment resulting from discriminatory hiring practices that exclude certain segments of the work force. Also, unemployment resulting from workers' inability or unwillingness to relocate in search of employment.

studio   Hotel or motel room with no bed but rather one or more couches that are used for sleeping.

study group   Charter or tour comprised solely of bona fide participants in an academic course of study.

subcontractor   *See* contractor.

subject to temporary accommodations   Term used mainly by Bermuda hotels. It indicates confirmation of space, but allows the hotel designated to arrange other accommodations in another hotel in the event space is not available.

subsidy   Direct or indirect governmental support of a private industry, as in government funding of aircraft research and airport construction.

subway   Underground, usually electric, railway in a large city. It may be called by various names. In London it is the *Underground* (colloquial *Tube*) and in Paris the *Metro*. *See also* train; elevated railway.

suggested itinerary   Preliminary itinerary provided by a travel agent or tour operator for a client's consideration. This generally shows routings and approximate times as well as recommended hotels and suggested sightseeing excursions.

suite   Accommodations that include two rooms, one for sleeping and another for sitting, as well as a private bath.

summer fare   Depending on the point of origin, the destination, or the route, the highest, lowest, or medium fare or rate of the year. *See* high season; low season.

sun over the foreyard   Shipboard expression meaning that it is time for a drink.

supplement   Additional charge for better accommodations, extra service, or the charge itself.

supplemental airline   Any airline authorized to offer charter service for passengers or cargo.

supplier   One who offers services or products for sale.

support services   Employee housing, fire and police protection, shopping areas, schools, and hospitals provided for destination areas, but not usually used by visitors.

suprastructure   Hotels and other visitor facilities, such as restaurants, entertainment facilities, shops. A destination area's facilities most clearly observable by the tourist.

surcharge   Add-on to a tour price, air fare, or other product or service, usually justified as a temporary but necessary method of coping with an extraordinary rise in supplier costs over which the supplier has no control; example: fuel surcharge. Also, an additional amount charged to a client who voluntarily selects better accommodations than those provided in a tour package.

surface carrier   Company or vehicle offering transportation by means other than aircraft, for example a bus, train, or ship.

survey   Research method of obtaining data on consumer decision-making and preferences. The survey method tends to use short answer questionnaires distributed in a nonrandom manner to persons agreeing to take part. Variations: in-flight, on board, direct-mail, paid attendant, audience.

T

tab   Slang expression for a customer's bill.

table d'hote   Fixed price meal. A complete meal as described on the menu for a set price, as distinguished from a la carte listings in which each item is priced separately.

table tent   Folded, printed card placed on restaurant tables and hotel room desks to promote special food items, events, or places of interest.

TAPSC   *See* International Passenger Ship Association.

tariff   1. Fare or rate from a supplier; 2. Class or type of fare or rate; 3. Published list of fares or rates from a supplier; 4. Official publication compiling fares or rates and conditions of service; 5. Any one or a combination of taxes or customs duty, applied to goods as they enter or leave a country.

tariff, confidential   Detailed schedule of wholesale rates, valid for a certain time period, given in confidence to travel agents. The rates are marked up to include a profit for the retailer, and paid by the customer as retail rates.

TC1, TC2, TC3   Traffic Conference Areas one, two, and three. *See* Traffic Conference Areas.

technical stop   Aircraft landing for purposes other than enplaning or deplaning passengers.

teleferic   Enclosed cabin attached to a motorized moving cable for transport between two points as in the case of a ski resort or nonroad access, attraction, or facility. Teleferics are two large cabins moving in opposite directions on the same cable system. Cabin lifts are smaller versions of the above. *See* cable transporters.

teleskis   Motorized moving cable with a bar or T-bar for one or more persons to hold or sit upon, providing transport. *See* cable transporters.

teletourist   *See* automatic guide.

tender   Craft used to transport passengers and crew from and to a ship anchored off.

terms and conditions   Paragraph or section of a transportation, tour, or other purchase contract that specifies what is and is not offered to the purchaser, and the conditions for permitting legal cancellation by either party.

territorial itinerary   *See* itinerary, international territorial.

theme park   Multiexperience area; often a destination in itself. Knotts Berry Farm is the United States' oldest theme park. Other examples are Disney World and Marriott's Great America.

third class   *See* railroad classes of service (Europe).

Third World   Loosely defined as the underdeveloped or emerging countries of the world, especially those of Africa and Asia.

through-plane service   Air transportation between two cities so that passengers can travel on the same aircraft even though the flight involves one or more intermediate stops.

throwaway   Item in the land portion of a tour that is rarely used. It is included in the tour package merely to qualify the passenger for a tour-basing fare.

TIAA   *See* Travel Industry Association of America.

TIC   *See* travel information center.

ticket   Written or printed contract document showing that the bearer is entitled to a service as specified by date, time, and other stated conditions, in consideration of the amount paid or to be paid by the customer. Specifically, in airline passage, *ticket* refers to the full set of documents (auditor's coupon, agent's coupon, flight(s) coupon), which authorizes carriage as specified.

ticket agent   Anyone authorized to take reservations and write airline tickets; employee of an air carrier responsible for same.

ticket, conjunction   Two or more tickets issued at the same time and in sequential order, which together constitute a single contract of carriage.

ticket, group   Ticket valid for more than one passenger.

ticket, reissued   Ticket that is rewritten due to necessary or desired changes in an air itinerary; issued in exchange for the original ticket.

ticket, single passenger   Ticket valid for one passenger.

ticket stock   Blank airline tickets; may be a carrier's own stock or standardized stock to be used to book passage on any U.S. or foreign airline member of ATC or IATA. Blank tickets become valid only after they have been completed and validated with a travel agency's stamp. *See also* validation; validator.

TIE   *See* Travel Industry for the Environment.

time deepening   Tendency to cram as many activities as possible into a given time period.

timesharing   Ownership of an individual dwelling unit in addition to a share of the common property for a specific period of time. *Right-to-use* timesharing allows the purchaser to occupy the unit for the specified time period per year for a specified number of years. The purchaser does not hold title and the ownership rights expire after the specified time. *Interval* ownership provides the purchaser with real estate; the title, equity buildup and taxes are the owner's, the property may be rented or sold as with any other real estate.

tip *See* gratuity.

tip-on Small piece of printed paper attached to menus or brochures to promote a special item or service.

to be assigned Usually refers to a steamship or cruise booking by which the line has guaranteed space but is unable to assign a specific cabin.

tollway *See* highway.

topography Physical features of any region, especially in map or chart form.

topper *See* pickup camper.

total design team Consulting team of architects, real estate analysts, accountants, interior designers, and other specialists that provides a client with a coordinated project, designed from the very beginning to meet the needs of the client and the intended customer.

total travel time Amount of time it actually takes to travel from one point to another, including all ground time along the way.

tour Any prearranged (usually prepaid) journey to one or more destinations and returning to the point of departure. Usually includes transportation, accommodations, meals, sightseeing and other components.

tour basing fare *See* fare.

tour brochure *See* brochure.

tour broker Person or company licensed by the Interstate Commerce Commission to organize and market motorcoach tours in the United States.

tour conductor *See* tour manager.

tour coupon Document used in exchange for accommodations, meals, sightseeing, and so forth. *See* coupon.

tour departure Date, time and location that marks the beginning of a particular travel program or tour.

tour desk 1. Desk, table, or counter-space often located in the lobby area of a hotel and staffed by a hotel employee for the purpose of answering questions, providing information on things to do, and solving a variety of guest problems; 2. Desk at an airline ticket office staffed by an airline employee who sells tours and packages to passengers.

tour director *See* tour manager.

tour escort *See* tour manager.

touring Subsystem of tourism that focuses on the needs of people while geographically mobile, including transportation facilities, availability of information, and the proximity of stopover attractions. From the standpoint of the tourist, the act or experience of briefly visiting a number of areas as part of a single round trip.

tourism Variously defined. Umbrella term for the variety of products and services offered and desired by people while away from home. Included are restaurants, accommodations, activities, natural and man-made attractions, travel agencies, government bureaus, transportation. Includes an awareness that this myriad of products and services are interrelated and interdependent. For example, an airline needs a destination which in turn needs everything from hotels to retail shops to a welcoming resident population. Also: 1. The relationship and phenomena associated with the journeys and temporary visits of people traveling primarily for leisure and recreation; 2. A subset of recreation; that form of recreation involving geographic mobility; 3. The industries and activities that provide and market the services needed for pleasure travel.

tourism activities   Any one or more of a variety of things for the tourist to do, see, and experience while enroute or while at a destination.

tourism, international   Defined by the World Tourism Organization as travel across international borders for more than 24 hours for the purpose of business or pleasure. Also, generally defined as travel for any peaceful reason or any duration short of permanency, necessitating the crossing of national borders.

tourismagnetic area   Place where tourism has become the major source of income and the major cultural influence. Also, an area that draws tourists.

tourism barriers   *See* barriers; barrier-free.

tourism caucus   *See* House Congressional Tourism Caucus; Senate Tourism Caucus.

tourism, cultural   Tourism that focuses upon the rich past of a people or areas as preserved and portrayed in monuments, historic sites, traditional architecture, and artifacts. As a planning strategy cultural tourism describes an attempt to create an enriching environment for resident and visitor alike, balancing the requirements of the tourist with those of the regional and national wellbeing, the business community, and the environment.

tourism, domestic   Use of tourism facilities within some legally-bordered area, usually a nation, by the residents of that area.

tourism facilities   Manmade elements of a tourism destination. *See* infrastructure and suprastructure.

tourism growth   Statistical increases in destination area accommodation units or increases in the number of visitors to an area.

tourism industry   Entire spectrum of government and business activities that provide and manage the needs, wants, and desires of the tourist. Includes agencies and groups seeking to promote tourism, the residents of destination areas, and educational institutions seeking to provide qualified industry personnel.

tourism, institutionalized   Broad category of tourism characterized by a relatively complete plan for all aspects of the travel experience, using established accommodations, transport, and attractions. *See also* mass tourism.

tourism, linear   *See* tourism, progressive.

tourism, noninstitutionalized   Broad category of tourism characterized by a relatively unorganized and highly individual form of travel experience.

tourism planning   Process of determining the future of tourism by the analysis of present facts, the identification of desired goals, and the establishment of strategies to obtain desired goals.

tourism policy   Plans, strategy, and actions of a decision-making body calculated to achieve identified, specific objectives relevant to tourism.

tourism product   1. Any one or some combination of the tourism goods and services available to the tourist; 2. The experiences and memories resulting from taking part in a tourism activity.

tourism, progressive   Also known as linear tourism, whereby tourism facilities and minidestination areas are strategically provided along a line through the country or region.

tourism, recreational   Subset of tourism activities which focuses on persons who are motivated to travel by their desire to participate in their favorite recreational activities in a new geographic setting, be it golf, tennis, hiking, and so forth.

tourism, rural   Type of tourism that bases its appeal and offered services on some aspect of the real or imagined rural, nonurban way of life: the vast, quiet, unrushed countryside, varieties of trees and animals, and so forth.

tourism, social   Government subsidized tourism, encouraging the availability of noncommercial tourism experiences for those who would otherwise be denied for financial or physical reasons. Tourism is seen as improving mental and physical health, as well as family relations. The term is more often used in Europe.

tourist   Someone 1. who has traveled at least 100 miles from home; 2. who stays overnight away from home; 3. who is travelling away from home primarily for pleasure (nonbusiness). Defined by the World Tourism Organization, a tourist is a temporary visitor staying at least twenty-four hours in a country visited for the purpose of leisure or business. The United Nations defines a tourist as one who spends more than one night and less than one year away from home for business or pleasure, excepting diplomats, military personnel, and enrolled students. Another definition: a tourist is any person travelling outside of his normal commuting radius for the purpose of pleasure or business. Most generally, a tourist is a person who has traveled away from home, is visiting other locations and does not plan to relocate or stay away from home permanently. *See* visitor.

tourist boom   Substantial increase in numbers of arriving visitors, with concomitant strain on facilities and services.

tourist card   Document, issued particularly by the countries of Central and South America, that permits the tourist to enter and depart the issuing country. *See also* visa.

tourist class   Accommodations or other facilities or services that are below first class.

tourist expenditures   Amount of money spent by tourists for their travel experiences. May be calculated as expenditures while at a destination or as a total, independent of where funds were spent. Includes transportation, lodging, food, gifts and incidentals, and entertainment.

tourist flow   Statistical measure of the volume and direction of movement of tourists into or out of an area, nation, or continent for a given period of time or as a trend.

tourist ghetto   1. Area in which tourists and tourist facilities are concentrated; 2. Destination area where tourists meet only other tourists or employees; 3. Proposed tourist developments in Third World countries designed to avoid conflict by keeping tourists separate from residents.

tourist home   Small, individually owned properties which offer accommodations to tourists. They are usually lower in cost than hotels or motels, and have a family atmosphere. The tourist home is usually in fact the home of its owner, a part of which is available as accommodations for nonfamily members. Also known as a guest house. *See also* boarding house.

tourist-host encounter   Meeting and interaction of tourists with residents of a destination area.

tourist hotel   Hotel offering accommodations with few if any private baths and limited services. Also referred to as an economy hotel or a second class hotel.

tourist office   *Government tourist office* is responsible for promoting tourism to the country it represents; a *state tourist office* is responsible for promoting tourism to its state. *See also* convention and visitors bureau.

tourist, personal   Person traveling for family related reasons (birth, death, birthdays, Christmas, etc.) rather than for pleasure or business.

tourist receipts   Amount of money spent by tourists in a given area during a specific time period.

tourist resources   Money, time, and personal desire necessary to become involved in a tourism experience. All other consumer products and services compete for one or more of these scarce resources.

tourist room   *See* rooming house.

tourist service   In international transport operations, *tourist service* is the generally-used term for coach service. *See* coach.

tourist tax   Any tax designed to be collected primarily from visitors in the form of a departure tax, entry tax, room tax, and so forth.

tourist trap   Derogatory term for a destination area or specific business establishment; place that has been overrun with tourists and offers very little in return for its high prices and poor service; appealing only to the unsophisticated.

tour leader   *See* tour manager.

tour manager   Person employed as the escort for tourists, usually for the entire travel experience, perhaps supplemented by local area guides. There exists no universally accepted standard for tour managers, but the International Association of Tour Managers (IATM) requires that a qualified tour manager have five years service in the position, during which the applicant must have escorted a minimum of ten independent or group tours annually. The terms *director, leader, escort, conductor,* and, in Europe, *courier* have the same meaning and are used interchangeably.

tour operator   *See* wholesale tour operator.

tour order   Form issued by a travel agent or airline to cover package tour ground arrangements (hotel, sightseeing, entertainment features, and so forth). The client normally exchanges the tour order for hotel and tour vouchers upon arrival at the destination.

tour organizer   Person who locates and creates groups that qualify for special rates offered by a prepaid tour. May be an outside sales representative of a travel agency.

tour package   Travel plan including most elements of a vacation such as transportation, accommodations, and sightseeing at a price which is lower than if the traveler purchased each service separately.

tour sales agent   Usually an airline employee, one who is responsible for selling tours and packages sponsored by the airline.

tour shell   Brochure containing graphics or illustrations but no copy, to be overprinted by travel agents and tour wholesalers.

tour talker   *See* automatic guide.

tour voucher   *See* coupon; exchange order; tour order.

tour wholesaler   *See* wholesale tour operator.

tout   Usually an area resident who lures or hounds a tourist into patronizing a certain hotel or shop.

TPPC   *See* Trans-Pacific Passenger Conference.

traffic   Clientele; customers.

Traffic Conference Areas   IATA divisions of the world for rate and rule-making purposes. Area one (TC1): North and South America and adjacent islands— Greenland, Bermuda, West Indies and Caribbean Islands, Hawaiian Islands, Midway, and Palmyra. Area Two (TC2): Europe (including USSR west of the Ural Mountains) and adjacent islands, Iceland, Azores, Africa and adjacent islands, Ascension Island, Middle East. Area Three (TC3): Asia and adjacent islands except parts included in Area Two, East Indies, Australia, New Zealand and adjacent islands, Pacific Ocean islands except those in Area One.

traffic density   Total amount or units of traffic density between two points, over a route, on a flight, or measured against any other reference.

trail   In tourism, usually a route that has been carefully selected and clearly marked with necessary legal permission for use as a right-of-way. Examples include bike, snowmobile, hiking, walking, sightseeing. Seasonality often provides for multiuse of the same trail.

transnational corporation   Business enterprise that owns or controls assets in two or more countries.

Transport Workers Union of America AFL-CIO   Trade union representing many United States airline employees.

train   A series of connected railway cars pushed or pulled by a locomotive. There are various types of trains and train services. *Local trains* serve small communities, or are used for commuting in larger cities; *express trains* are fast, long-distance trains with limited stops, often requiring reservations and payment of a supplement over the normal fare. *Trans-Europ Express (TEE) trains* are fast day trains connecting important European cities. Several European countries have special names for their fast, limited stop luxury trains; these include the *Rapido* trains of Italy and the *Talgo* trains of Spain. The *Metroliner* is a high-speed train operating on short and intermediate intercity routes within the United States. Until recently the fastest train in the world was the *Bullet* train of Japan which reached a speed of 130 mph. In 1981 a new electric train goes into service in France which will cruise initially at 160 mph and eventually at 190 mph. Many crack trains carry names, of which the *Orient Express* was the most famous; other examples of name trains include *Train Bleu* (Paris-Nice); *Sud Express* (Paris-Lisbon); *The Flying Scotsman* (London-Edinburgh); *Indian-Pacific* (Sydney-Perth); *Blue Train* (Pretoria-Durban); *Canadian* (Montreal-Vancouver); and the *Broadway Limited* (New York-Chicago). *See also* elevated railway; subway.

Trans-Atlantic Passenger Steamship Conference (TAPSC)   *See* International Passenger Ship Association.

transfer   Service provided for arriving or departing travelers to transport them from an air, sea, or rail terminal to their hotel, or between one terminal and another terminal. A standard element of an inclusive tour.

translator   Multilingual person provided by a hotel, tour operator or other business as a service to customers for the purpose of facilitating communication among persons who do not speak a common language. Also, the general name for a new generation of electronic machines which translate a basic vocabulary of one language into another by means of a visual display or audibly.

Trans-Pacific Passenger Conference (TPPC)   Promotional and regulatory organization of major steamship companies which offer trans-Pacific passenger services.

transportation taxes   Inclusive term for all taxes related to transportation including departure, arrival, excess baggage, and ticket taxes.

travel   To make a journey from one place to another place by any means, for any purpose, with or without return to the original point of departure.

travel agency   An establishment accredited by the Air Traffic Conference, the International Air Transport Association, and other conferences, which gives information, arranges reservations, and sells tickets to travelers. Also called a *travel bureau.*

travel agent Person, firm, or corporation qualified to sell tours, cruises, transportation, hotel accommodations, meals, transfers, sightseeing, and all other elements of travel to the public as a service.

Travel and Tourism Research Association (TTRA) Professional membership society of specialists in travel industry market research. Formerly The Travel Research Association.

travelator Level-ground version of the escalator. Where the escalator is a moving platform carrying people up or down, the travelator assists pedestrians in their travel from one part of an area to another, be it a destination area or an airport. Also known as a *moving sidewalk*.

travel directory *See* guidebook.

travelers check Form of negotiable currency that must be countersigned when used. Issued by some banks and a number of large travel companies, they offer a welcome degree of security over cash for the traveler.

Travel Industry Association of America (TIAA) Nonprofit association of government organizations and private companies formed to promote travel to and within the United States. Formerly the Discover America Travel Organization (DATO), the new name signifies an integration and expansion of promotional and research efforts.

Travel Industry for the Environment (TIE) Group concerned with encouraging awareness of the delicate interdependence between tourism and the environment.

travel information center Information office, often government funded, located on major highways, in city centers or transportation terminals for use by travelers.

travel merchant Retail travel agent who places great emphasis upon the high volume merchandising/sales of a limited product variety.

travel multiplier *See* multiplier effect.

travel price index (TPI) Composite statistic compiled by the U.S. Travel Data Center, which measures the seasonally unadjusted cost of transportation, food, lodging, and other tourism goods and services purchased by American travelers for a given time period, usually annually.

trip In common usage, the term *trip* tends to include both the going and returning portions of a journey. In airline usage, it is important to distinguish whether *trip* is used in a one-way or round-trip sense. Published statistics on average length of air trips are almost always one-way distances, since it is virtually impossible to determine from reported data what the round-trip distance is. Fares, on the other hand, are sometimes quoted as one-way prices and, at other times as round-trip prices; the round-trip price is not always equal to twice the one-way price.

triple Room or other facility occupied by three persons or designated to be used by three persons.

tropics 1. Either of the two parallels of latitude corresponding 23 degrees 7 minutes north and south of the equator; the northern one is called the Tropic of Cancer and the southern one the Tropic of Capricorn. The region between the two tropics is called the *torrid zone*; 2. An area characteristic of the climates between the tropics.

trunk carrier A major United States airline with an extensive route system.

truth-in-advertising legislation Legislation that requires a business to increase its accurate disclosure to the customer of what is, in fact, being purchased. Restaurants are most affected by *truth-in-menu,* that is, accurate descriptions of the meat type, country of origin, and so forth, Travel service suppliers are often required to correct promotional techniques that imply a guarantee of some sort where none exists. *See also* accuracy in menu.

truth-in-menu *See* truth-in-advertising legislation.

TS Turbine Ship

TSS Turbine Steamship

TTRA *See* Travel and Tourism Research Association.

turista General term for a number of gastrointernal illnesses with symptoms ranging from mild to severe stomach cramps, vomiting, and fever. Recognized in some countries as due to specific water-borne bacteria. Many tourists experience turista as a consequence of change from normal habits in eating volume, selection, and overindulgence. Slang expressions for this condition abound.

turnover 1. The number of times during a given period that a business's inventory (food, liquor) is replaced because of sales; 2. Number of times a restaurant seat is occupied by a new customer in a given meal period.

twin Hotel room having two single beds for use by two persons.

twin double Hotel or motel room accommodating two, three, or four persons, provided with two double beds.

U

UATP *See* Universal Air Travel Plan.

U-drive *See* self drive.

UFTAA *See* Universal Federation of Travel Agents Associations.

ugly American Negative stereotype of U.S. citizens abroad, in response to their perceived cultural insensitivity.

UIC *See* International Union of Railways.

underdeveloped *See* developing country.

UNESCO *See* United Nations Educational Scientific and Cultural Organization.

unit Free-standing individual place of business, especially when part of a company with more than one place of business—a multiunit company. Also, an individual accommodation—hotel room, condominium apartment, or resort cottage.

United Nations Educational Scientific and Cultural Organization (UNESCO) International body concerned, among other things, with tourism as a strategy alternative for economic development and as an agent of social influence and change.

United States Tour Operators' Association (USTOA) Trade association of tour operators.

United States Travel Data Center (USTDC) Independent nonprofit educational and research organization charged with improving the quality of travel and tourism research in the United States.

United States Travel Data Service (USTDS) Cooperative association of government and business representing the travel industry by conducting, compiling, and disseminating information on travel patterns and trends.

United States Travel Service (USTS) Agency of the Department of Commerce responsible for promoting travel to the United States from abroad.

Universal Air Travel Plan (UATP) Airline-sponsored credit card system.

Universal Federation of Travel Agents Associations (UFTAA) International association of national travel agency trade associations.

unspoiled Advertising term with no agreed-on definition. Generally taken to mean uncommercialized, informal, and not frequented by tourists.

upgrade To change to a better class of service, be it in an aircraft, hotel or motel accommodation, or entire tour package.

uplift ratio Government identified statistical formula used to regulate a balance between outbound charter traffic and inbound traffic by foreign carriers.

urban sprawl Often undesired expansion of high-density urban-like developments from a central city into surrounding rural areas.

USTDC *See* United States Travel Data Center.

USTOA *See* United States Tour Operators' Association.

USTS *See* United States Travel Service.

utopia Literally, "no place"; an imaginary community where social, political and economic aspects approach perfection.

V

vacancy Availability of commercial accommodation space or a seating space at a limited-seating function or facility, as at a dinner, a cruise, or a theater.

vacation Time away from employment; paid time off from work.

vacation home Secondary residence used for relatively brief periods during specific seasons.

vacation savings plan Service provided by a savings institution whereby a person is offered an incentive for depositing money in the form of travel or tour packages. The person is notified when the necessary amount for the travel package selected is reached.

vacation trip Tourism experience that uses discretionary time and money for travel that includes fun and pleasure.

vaccination Preventive medical practice of inoculating a person with one or a series of modified viruses so as to render the person immune to specific diseases. A person's country of origin specifies the inoculations that are required or recommended, depending on the area of the world to be visited.

validation Creation of a legal ticket by imprinting it with a die plate stamp.

validator Hand operated machine, fitted with a specific carrier or travel agency die plate, that validates ticket stock.

validity dates Dates for which a flight, tour package, fare, or rate is valid.

value added tax (VAT) Government imposed tax based on the value added at each stage of the production and distribution of a product or service.

vandalism Willful destruction of property.

variable costs Business operating expenses that increase or decrease in direct relationship with the number of customers; for example, laundry, food, and employee wages.

VAT *See* value added tax.

vending machines Machines that display and automatically provide one or a long list of items for a customer at any time without the need or expense of service personnel. Snack foods and cigarettes are frequently sold in this way.

vendor Supplier, usually of one product or of a small variety of products. *See also* purveyor.

verification Process of substantiating the truth or correctness of what has been presented as true, as in the case of room reservations, credit card use, or proof of citizenship.

vertical integration Predicted consequence of CAB regulation. An example would be an economic impetus for airlines and large suppliers to own, operate and possibly control other levels of the travel industry.

vertical travel 1. Elevator or lift; 2. The concept that transportation is involved and that a facility can offer diverse experiences and uses, each at a different level but all within one building or structure.

vice   Wide range of behavior, both legal and illegal, that is disapproved of but often permitted, at least in certain areas or for certain segments of a population.

vice squad   Special unit of law enforcement charged with stopping, or at least containing, prostitution, gambling, and other vice activities in an area.

video habitat   Self-contained entertainment experience module offering wrap-around video images, holograms, stereo sound, and so forth, for use by one or more people. Suggested as a future supplement, alternative, or competitor to tourism, especially business travel.

villa   *See* individual housing.

visa   Official authorization, permitting for some specific time, travel to and within a specific country granting the visa. The authorization is added to a person's passport. *See also* tourist card.

visitor   Usually used interchangeably with *tourist* but stressing the temporary nature of the stay at one or more destinations with no designation of the reason(s) for traveling. *Tourist* tends to highlight the pleasure experiences and the assumed use of commercial facilities. In some cases the word *visitor* is preferred over that of *tourist,* especially where the latter term has a negative connotation.

visitor and convention bureau   *See* convention and visitors bureau.

visitor participation   Planning consideration; encouraging the visitor to take an active part in the situation, activity, or event, rather than simply observe.

vista   Panoramic view of a beautiful countryside or a dynamic urban skyline obtainable from a specific location or lookout point. *Vista planning* is an area design strategy intended to provide users, especially pedestrians, with panoramic views and open-area visual experiences.

volume incentive   Some percentage of extra commission paid as a bonus for volume sales.

voyage   Journey of relatively significant distance predominantly by watercraft.

voucher   *See* coupon; exchange order; tour order.

VTOL   *See* aircraft.

W

Wagon Lits   Company operating railroad sleeping cars in Europe.

waitlist   List of passengers who are waiting confirmation on a flight, ship, tour, and so forth, that is sold out.

walk in   Guest or customer who comes to a property without having made a reservation.

wanderer   *See* drifter.

Warsaw Convention   The original international agreement signed in Warsaw in 1929 governing liability for damages for death, injury, or loss to passengers, baggage, and merchandise. The 1968 Montreal Agreement amended the original, limiting per-person liability to $75,000 and waiving the right of defense.

WATA   *See* World Association of Travel Agents.

watering hole   Slang expression for a bar, cocktail lounge, or other commercial establishment dispensing alcoholic beverages.

welcome center   Information center located in areas or on routes frequented by visitors, funded by government or jointly with businesses.

wet lease   Rental of a vehicle, complete with crew and all other operational necessities. *See also* dry lease.

wheelchair request   Airline codes for needed wheelchair service: WCHC: passenger completely immobile; WCHR: passenger can go up and down steps and make own way to seat; WCHS: passenger cannot go up or down steps, but can make own way to seat.

wholesaler   *See* wholesale tour operator.

wholesale tour operator   The terms *packager, wholesale tour operator, tour operator, tour wholesaler,* and *wholesaler* are often used interchangeably. In almost every case, the company acting as a wholesaler also operates the tours it creates or packages. Specifically, the wholesaler arranges tour packages, that is, contracts with hotels, ground transportation companies, attractions, and other components, thereby assembling the ingredients of a package tour. A wholesaler produces the brochures for distribution to individuals through travel agents and airline ticket offices. Earnings are derived from commissions and a markup on the net cost of the components. Tours and packages are marketed through travel agents (who receive a commission from the wholesaler) and airlines.

wide body   *See* aircraft.

winter fare/rate   Depending on the point of origin, the destination, or the route, the highest, lowest, or medium priced fare of the year. Winter rates for hotels and attractions tend to follow the same seasonal pattern as do transportation fares. *See* high season; low season.

World Association of Travel Agents (WATA)   International association of retail travel agents.

World Bank   International investment institution that makes and guarantees loans for worthwhile development projects, including tourism.

world class   Unofficial designation implying that the institution or business provides a level of luxury and range of services equal to any in the world.

World Health Organization (WHO)   United Nations agency that keeps track of communicable diseases throughout the world, and advises governments on recommended vaccination requirements for travelers.

World Tourism Organization (WTO)   The International Union of Official Travel Organizations (IUOTO) was created in 1925 for the purpose of promoting and developing tourism in the interest of economic, social, and cultural progress of all nations. It was a member association of all national tourism organizations. The IUOTO no longer exists, as the World Tourism Organization, officially ratified in 1974, superseded it in membership and purpose.

WTO   *See* World Tourism Organization.

X

xenophobia   Psychological condition of fear and contempt for strangers and foreigners.

Y

yacht   a sail, steam, or motor vessel used for pleasure.

yield   Average amount of revenue earned per revenue passenger mile; computed by dividing total passenger revenue by the total number of passenger miles flown.

youth hostel   *See* hostel.

youth market   Description of a market segment involving single persons 18 to 25 years of age.

Z

zoning laws   Ordinances or laws passed by cities and towns restricting the use of specified lands to exclude or include certain activities. Part of the destination area planning process.